FULL FLEDGE

UNDERSTANDING THE POWER OF FAITH

Dr. Angela Roberson

Full Fledge- Understanding the Power of Faith
Dr. Angela Roberson, CEO& FOUNDER
Heart2Heart Ministries International Foundation
501c3nonprofit
e-mail: heart2heart.ar@gmail.com

Daughter of the King Television International Network
website: dktv.org

20 PEARLS PRESS
Jocelyn.mull@gmail.com

First printed August 2023

ISBN: 9798862241044

DEDICATION

Prophetess Angelique Lynn

God bless you for pouring into my life and seeing this book come to fruition. I honor the GOD in you. The power of GOD moved in me the night you prophesied about the book's name and the first and last chapters.

ACKNOWLEDGMENTS

I honor my father, Willie Roberson, and my mother, Marguerite Turner.

My Great-grandmother, Corine Branch, and Grandmother, Vera O'Neil, and Auntie Anginette Simmons, thank God for all the life lessons you inspired in me, creating standards for living, I still follow today.

God gave me three special gifts, my three boys, Brian, Mark, and Angelo, you have made your Mommy proud of you.

My loving cousin and friend, Ashana -Bri Simmons I am so proud of the strides toward excellence in your life. Thank you for your encouragement. We stand in the gap for each other.

Pastor Charles Price and Dr. Jocelyn Mull-Wouldn't take anything for my journey.

To all additional family and friends, thank you for supporting me during this journey of writing the book.

My two spiritual daughters, Prophetess Danilla Smith, and Simone Williams, Prophet James Hewett continue loving GOD with all your heart and with all thy soul, and with all thy and with all thy mind. He has begun a great work in you. **Matthew 22:37-39,**

> *Jesus said unto him, "Thou shalt love the Lord thy God with all thy heart, and with all thy soul, and with all thy mind. This is the first and great commandment. And the second is like unto it, Thou shalt love thy neighbour as thyself."*

FORWARD

By Pastor Emeritus Charles Walter Price

I've had the pleasure of talking with Dr. Angela Roberson, and I've found her to signify why she's qualified to write this book; because of all that she's gone through, she has the *"Fear of the Lord"* in her.

Psalm 111:10

> *"The fear of the Lord is the beginning* (foundation) *of* (true) *wisdom: a good understanding have all they that do his commandments: his praise endureth forever."*

We know that in this context, the word fear does not mean to "be afraid of" but rather "to have reverence for" or "to revere" This is mankind's duty: to have reverence for God and to keep (do) His commandments.

Dr. Roberson used her hard life as a tool to have faith in God, but! She understood that you needed more than just faith to overcome this world, you needed wisdom, the wisdom of God. She understands to take God seriously in this way is the foundation of wisdom. To be wise is to have a clear understanding of how to obey God's commands in specific situations in her life.

Psalm 111:10 shows us how to become wise: "Fear of the LORD is the foundation of true wisdom." This core truth, which appears elsewhere in Scripture (Prov. 9:10, for example), reminds us that wisdom is not something we gain on our own.

TABLE OF CONTENTS

INTRODUCTORY PRAYER

God gracefully breaks us all, so He can take us higher. Father, we find our way through worship, prayer, and supplication by refocusing our minds on the things of **FATHER GOD**. For our grace comes through faith. For we must have faith to accept the grace that our Heavenly Father has given us. Lord. Your mercy is because we deserve to die, but Jesus, died on your behalf. For You had compassion for us, for the debt we owed, but could not pay, we needed someone to wash our sin away.

In **John 15:15-18,**

"Henceforth I call you not servants; for the servant knoweth not what his lord doeth: but I have called you friends; for all things that I have heard of my Father I have made known unto you.¹⁶ Ye have not chosen me, but I have chosen you, and ordained you, that ye should go and bring forth fruit, and that your fruit should remain: that whatsoever ye shall ask of the Father in my name, he may give it to you. ¹⁷ These things I command you, that ye love one another. ¹⁸ If the world hates you, ye know that it hated me before it hated you."

Father God, I am humbled because Your Son, Jesus, chose me as an Apostle. He strengthened me and gave me the courage to WIN. In this season of my life, I stand firm on the Word of the LORD.

Habakkuk 2:1-4 says,

"I will stand upon my watch, and set me upon the tower, and will watch to see what he will say unto me, and what I shall answer when I am reproved:² And the Lord answered me, and said, "Write the vision and make it plain upon tables, that he may run that readeth it. ³ For the vision is yet for an appointed time, but at the end, it shall speak, and not lie: though it tarries, wait for it; because it will surely come, it will not tarry. ⁴ Behold, his soul which is lifted up is not upright in him: but the just shall live by his faith."

We must manifest our vision. Write it down and make it plain. We are to work, the work of the one who sent us. **Ephesians 1** says, *"It is HE who established us and manifested HIS Spirit in us to do the will of God."* I realized I am because HE chose me to be an effective witness. In every struggle I experienced, GOD healed me.

"I must work the works of him that sent me, while it is day: the night cometh, when no man can work. 5 As long as I am in the world, I am the light of the world." **John 9:4-5**

The more I believed His Word, the more God began to reveal Himself to me. Surrendering to His Will empowered me to stand on His Word. Miracles, Signs, and Wonder.

CHAPTER 1

STRUGGLES

1 Corinthians 10:13 says,

"There hath no temptation taken you, but such as is common to man: but God is faithful, who will not suffer you to be tempted above that ye are able; but will with the temptation also make a way to escape, that ye may be able to bear it."

I turned eighteen after I graduated from my senior year of high school. I was so excited because everything was moving into place for me. I was very interested in Media and television. I had hoped to go to college and learn my craft.

After graduation, I got scarlet fever. I woke up the following day and went into the restroom, and my legs were locked. I fell, and I was unable to get up off the floor. I screamed for my dad, and he came running. He helped me get dressed and called my mother, notifying her that I was going to the Hospital.

My Mother had to help me. A side-effect of scarlet fever is paralysis. Since I was unable to help myself, Mom came and took me to stay with her. I couldn't walk for a year. I needed help around the clock, so I stayed in the middle room in my great-grandmother's house.

I talked to the Lord daily. I had to fix my face to express myself with clarity of thought. I dared to say to God, "Why am I still here? What am I supposed to do?

Why don't you take me if I am not able to walk? What good am I to anyone? I can't even help myself. This was my time to shine and go to college. Lord, can you hear me?

This is where my first faith was built. The doctors were saying I may never walk again. I watched my grandmother and Mother as they took care of me, they continued praying throughout my room for healing to take place. They honestly believed that God could intervene. They spoke God's promises over my life. However, my great-grandmother, Corrine, owned a lot of property. She lived in the front house. I stayed in the middle room. I remained here until I was physically able to walk and take care of myself. I survived one of the major side effects of scarlet fever and can walk and navigate life.

As my grandmother and mother were taking care of me, their lives were a testimony to God in every way. His love, His goodness, His grace, His forgiveness, His righteousness, His self-lessness, perfect living examples of the Word of God,

Luke 18:27 says,

"The things that are impossible with people are possible with God."

It's a fact, that God raised Jesus from the dead (**Romans 8:11).** In other words, if God has the power to raise Jesus from the dead, then He has the power to solve your impossible problems. It's impossible for God to lie, so what He said in **Luke 18:27** is true, or He would seek to exist.

Isaiah 55:11 says,

"For as the rain cometh down, and the snow from heaven, and returneth not thither, but watereth the earth, and maketh it bring forth and bud, that it may give seed to the sower, and bread to the eater: [11] So shall my word be that goeth forth out of my mouth: it shall not return unto me void, but it shall accomplish that which I please, and it shall prosper in the thing whereto I sent it."

This scripture means that God's Words are true. When He talks, His words *accomplish* His intended purpose. The Word of the LORD has Dunamis (power, potential, or ability), and it never *fails* in His intended purpose.

"It is an irrevocable word. Man must eat his words, sometimes, and unsay his say. He would perform his engagement, but he cannot. It is not that he is unfaithful, but that he is unable. Now, this is never so with God. His words never return to him void. Go, find ye the snowflakes winging their way like white doves back to heaven! Go, find the drops of rain rising upward like diamonds flung up from the hand of a mighty man to find a lodging place in the cloud from which they fell! Until the snow and the rain return to heaven and mock the ground which they promised to bless, the word of God shall never return to him void." (Spurgeon)

I survived one of the major side effects of scarlet fever and can walk and navigate life. I am on my own now. Miraculously, God healed me. I was smiling from ear to ear because God favored me. I realize God hears your prayers. My family continued in prayer day and night, As I listened, I was strengthened in my mind, heart, and soul.

I can remember when I was living in Compton. I had my place for me and my son Brian. I told my family that I was having a baby. We lived with my father until I got a place of my own. My son's father was named Brian. We couldn't stay with him because he went to jail for selling drugs. He was imprisoned for nine years. The sad part about this is that his father, Brian, was away from my son Brian for most of his childhood.

I was wrong again.

I was going to the reggae club where I met Anthony. I started dating him, but he was so jealous. I was young; my son Brian was about three years old. He was very abusive towards me. He started hitting and punching me.

I was wrong again.

I remember dating Anthony. I would see him at the club. He watched every move I made while another man tried to talk to me. I would Sneak outside to give them my number. One night, Anthony came over. He had on a long coat. Brian was in the bedroom sleeping. I shut the door. Anthony pulled out this big old gun to instill fear in me. I was in shock and didn't know what he would do.

He put the gun dead in my face and said, ***"If I catch you giving anybody else your number, I'm going to kill you."*** Then he forced me to have sex with him.

I was traumatized.

I went to my son's room to see if he was still sleeping. Thank God he was in the room with the door shut. He was sound asleep, oblivious to what was going on in the next room.

I thought to myself, what have I gotten myself into? This man was crazy! So, the next morning, he left before Brian got up. I knew that this relationship was not going to last because I had become afraid of him.

I remember talking to him on the phone one night. I told him that I no longer wanted to be in a relationship. He said," Do you think you could end it with me that easily?" I often went to my Auntie's house to avoid him.

I was wrong again.

One night, my girls and I were hanging out on Crenshaw Boulevard. This nice-looking brother in an AMG Mercedes Benz walked up to me and said, ***"You look good. How can I help you?"*** I thought to myself, ***"Give me all of your money."*** I gave him my number, and he called me the next day. We started going out. He seemed cool in the beginning.

He was abusive over time. It came out that he was so jealous, and it didn't make any sense. He started trying to fight me.

He would give me all types of things. Money was no issue for him. But he was just so jealous. Eric didn't want me to go anywhere or do anything. One night, I was going out with my cousin. We were in the car, getting ready to pull off. He began to shoot at the car. I was so scared.

He told me to get out of the vehicle. He yanked me out and started punching me, hitting me in the head and chest. He choked on me. I never made it to the party. I went back home and cried.

I was wrong again.

I couldn't take it anymore. I didn't care about the money or cars anymore. It was just too much for me. I needed to get out of that relationship. I began praying. I didn't even know God in that way, but my great-grandmother taught me how to pray. She said, ***"Talk to God and tell Him what you feel in your heart."***

Psalms 34:18 says,

> *"The LORD is nigh unto them that are of a broken heart; and saveth such as be of a contrite spirit."*

I cried out to God to stop this band of chaos and confusion in my life. All I ever wanted was a real relationship where a man could me as I did him. I was hurting inside, not realizing that God could hear every word I uttered.

Psalm 77:1-3 says

> *"I cried unto God with my voice, even unto God with my voice; and he gave ear unto me. [2] In the day of my trouble I sought the Lord: my sore ran in the night and ceased not: my soul refused to be comforted. [3] I remembered God, and was troubled: I complained, and my spirit was overwhelmed. Selah".*

I can stand here before you today and say from my heart that God lends His ear to the cries of individuals in their times of sorrow, for He did it for me.

I stayed at my Auntie's house for a month. Eric came to talk to me outside. We were in the parking lot, and he pulled a gun out and began hitting me with it. I went down to my knees, and he said, ***"If you move, I will blow your head off."*** I was bleeding. I just began to call on Jesus. He needed something to drink, so he went across the street. I ran up the stairs to my aunt's apartment. I got inside, and he shot the whole apartment building up. We all got down on the floor to take cover. My Auntie called 911, and the Police came out. He went to jail that night.

I was wrong again

I met a man named Mac, and we became Full-fledged good friends. We used to talk a lot about life. We were not intimate at all. He would give me money, and I didn't know what to say when he bought me two Porsches. I found out that he was pretending to be a good man. Mac was a psychopath. He was trying to keep up with me.

He spent a lot of time contacting one of my cousins to get me to come home. Mac told her that he had bought me a new BMW.

I went home, and he picked me up to get the car, but then he took me to a field and shoved a gun down my throat. He busted my lip. I was pleading for the Lord to help me. I was crying so much that he took me back to my car. I realized that the enemy can't stand it when you call on the Lord. I called my mother and father. Mac was arrested for running a chop shop. Shortly after that, he went to prison for running a chop shop with stolen cars.

I keep saying, ***"I Am Wrong Again"***. Sometimes, our own (my) mistakes are a <u>reason for trials and tribulations</u> that happen in our lives. We are to grow in faith and get stronger in the Lord so we can make fewer mistakes. As a child grows and wiser, we will do the same in Christ. Ways to help learn from mistakes are praying continually, walking by the Spirit, continuing to meditate on the Word of God, putting on the full armor of God, being humble, trusting the Lord with all your heart, and not leaning on your own understanding.

I was wrong again.

Romans 5:3-6 says,

"And not only so, but we glory in tribulations also: knowing that tribulation worketh patience; [4] And patience, experience; and experience, hope: [5] And hope maketh not ashamed; because the love of God is shed abroad in our hearts by the Holy Ghost which is given unto us. [6] For when we were yet without strength, in due time Christ died for the ungodly".

Mac was Belizean. They shipped him back to Belize and made him a menace to society. He couldn't come back to the States anymore.

I went on with my life. I then met my two other sons' father. He was working as a Crowd Manager at the Academy of Motion Pictures, doing good for himself.

As time went on, we lived well; we were like best friends. When you saw him, you saw me. This man had my back, but as time went by, he got into it with one of the Movie Directors at his job. They blackballed him. He got fired at that time. I believe he went into a depression when his cousin had him come out to Spokane. That's when everything started going downhill.

We started having problems in the relationship. He started selling to get money because we were used to a certain amount of money. We broke up after a year and a half. We got back together, and this is when I became pregnant with this little Mark. He stayed with me. Mark went back to Spokane.

One night, he called me and said, ***"Baby, I can't live without you."*** I had just gotten my house and was working well at the County Hospital Harbor UCLA Medical Center when he returned to California to ask me to marry him.

Later, he began acting differently. Sometimes controlling and verbally abusive some days. I didn't want to return home from work. He was a good lover, But I didn't want to sleep with him anymore; he would force himself on me. This time, I got pregnant with Angelo, and I had made up my mind that I wanted a divorce. I still loved Mark, but I couldn't take it anymore.

The marriage was over. I sold my house in 2008 and moved in with my grandma to get myself back in order. He would come by every day, trying to convince me to take him back. I just couldn't, I knew it would be the same. So, he permanently moved back to Spokane. Amazingly, we decided to co-parent during summer breaks. He was a good father to my sons.

I was wrong again.

So, the next year, I started going on the motorcycle set that had never been there before. It was cool because now I have started to like having fun and parties. One day, I was out there and told my cousin I wanted to start a club for women. I spoke to some of my friends. I knew how to get everything started. He told me I needed to get ten members to start. I had ten members in less than twenty-four hours.

> **WILD WOMEN QUOTE**
> *I am just a Woman trying to live in a world that is gradually losing it's understanding of what it means to be a human being... - Shikoba.*
> kimberly montague

When I went before the board, Heart 2 Heart Compton Social Club was put on the map. It became the sister club to the male component Rare Breed. I started dating Vice President <u>K-D.</u> We dated for about two years.

I met his mother and started going to all their family functions. The women created problems due to jealousy and envy. He believed them. So, our relationship came to an end.

I was wrong again.

A year later, at a Black and Red dance, I <u>met RB</u> Fine; that's the only word I can use for that brother. He walked over to me and asked me to dance. The next is history. Let me tell you, it was a love connection, love at first sight. We could not stop dancing and talking, I used to be a good talker.

However, I am quiet today. I want to ensure that I am not using the same ways I had in the world. We would talk for hours. I fell so in love with him. He would come to spend time with me. We would look into each other's eyes.

It was like a Love story.

I can't deny it. I remember one day, a prophetess at my job began to tell me about the Lord and how God was calling me to Him. I had a picture of me in Hawaii with a rainbow around my head. My Mom and I had traveled together. The prophetess said, ***"There's a calling in your life."*** My question to myself was, "How could this woman tell me God called me and I didn't know Him as my Savior?"

This was indeed strange to me; this I did not understand. I did not know our Lord said, "I have called you by your name. You are mine". That means He fully knows who we are and claims us as His own (**Isaiah 43:1**, *"I have called thee by thy name; thou art mine."*). Most translations of this verse say, *"called you by name"* or *"called you by your name."* Either way, you choose to translate it; this is a declaration of knowing and caring on a deep, personal level.

Let's just stop for a minute and look at a few things the book of Isaiah is telling us. God has a special and unique claim upon us because He is our Creator.

Isaiah 43:7 says,

> *"Everyone called by My name and created for My glory, whom I have indeed formed and made."*

Isaiah 43:15 says,

> *"I am the LORD, your Holy One, the Creator of Israel, and your King."*

Isaiah 43:21 says,

> *"The people I formed for Myself will declare My praise."*

Prophetess Regina said, ***"The rainbow was a covenant with God."***

Genesis 9:13-17 New King James Version says,

*"I set My **rainbow** in the cloud, and it shall be for the sign of the **covenant** between Me and the earth. ¹⁴ It shall be, when I bring a cloud over the earth, that the **rainbow** shall be seen in the cloud; ¹⁵ and I will remember My **covenant** which is between Me and you and every living creature of all flesh; the waters shall never again become a flood to destroy all flesh. ¹⁶ The **rainbow** shall be in the cloud, and I will look on it to remember the everlasting **covenan**t between God and every living creature of all flesh that is on the earth." ¹⁷ And God said to Noah, "This is the sign of the **covenant** which I have established between Me and all flesh that is on the earth."*

Prophetess Regina wanted me to show BJ the picture of me and the rainbow. I learned that BJ was a Prophet, and she was a Prophetess. In my mind, I wanted to bow out gracefully. Yet, we did go to the gift shop. She told BJ that this was the one whom she was ministering to on the job about God.

When BJ looks at the picture he stands up from the seated position and says, ***"There is a calling on your life."*** In my mind, I said**, *"Here we go again."*** He told me to go to the lake. Regina was trying to **convert** my life to God. She told me my time was running out.

From that point on I seriously tried to stay away from them. However, I did like the Motorcycle Set. I was having fun. Regina did come to the Emergency Room to tell me God said, ***"I didn't have much time, and I needed to make a decision."***

I could prophesy to people who wanted to commit suicide or were emotionally distressed. I would find myself being a word of hope for many people on the motorcycle set. It was unusual for some people to see me helping other women deal with various life issues. I became the most sought-after woman on the motorcycle set to help women solve life issues.

So as not to get you confused: ***How can a believer live in sin yet be able to operate as though they weren't? Why would God allow this?***

According to His Word,

Romans 11:29 says,

"For the gifts and calling of God are without repentance."

***"Without repentance* (are irrevocable)"**

This means that if God had called you, He wouldn't change His mind about what He has called you to do. If God has called you, that calling on your life is still there, whether you choose to be or not to be obedient. Also, If God gave you a gift along a certain line—that gift is still there! **We must walk the way of Holiness.**

I have always had a heart for helping people. I love seeing people move forward and get the things out of the life God promised them. It has always been a struggle for me. People were constantly coming towards me.

I could never understand why I had to endure so much pain. God began to reveal a lot of things to me from childhood, family, and friends. What do you do when you have been hated for no reason, and you love people with all your heart?

I cried many nights from being mishandled, wondering why this happened to me.

But why not? My purpose was a threat to Satan's kingdom, and I had to understand it. I should be dead, but by the grace of God, I am still here.

I Am Still Here, MY TREASURY OF SCRIPTURES

1 Corinthians 15:10 says,

"But by the grace of God, I am what I am: and his grace which was bestowed on me was not in vain; but I labored more abundantly than they all: yet not I, but the grace of God which was with me."

Ephesians 2:7-10 says,

"That in the ages to come he might shew the exceeding riches of his grace in his kindness toward us through Christ Jesus. 8 For by grace are ye saved through faith; and that not of yourselves: it is the gift of God: 9 Not of works, lest any man should boast. 10 For we are his workmanship, created in Christ Jesus unto good works, which God hath before ordained that we should walk in them."

Some of the abuse I've had to suffer should've left me in a place of darkness and unforgiveness. Yet, I rise full of hope and faith because I know God is with me even in my struggles.

God told me in **Isaiah 41:10-13,**

> *"Fear thou not; for I am with thee be not dismayed; for I am thy God: I will strengthen thee; yea, I will help thee; yea, I will uphold thee with the right hand of my righteousness. 11 Behold, all they that were incensed against thee shall be ashamed and confounded: they shall be as nothing, and they that strive with thee shall perish. 12Thou shalt seek them, and shalt not find them, even them that contended with thee: they that war against thee shall be as nothing, and as a thing of naught. 13 For I the LORD thy God will hold thy right hand, saying unto thee, Fear not; I will help thee."*

I am still rejoicing in the Word of God. He is with me, loves and cares for me regardless of my circumstances. God told me not to fear. I started posting scriptures on my wall to recite daily.

Now, I am living in one of my grandmother's houses on Tarrant Street. It was given to me by her. I moved in and stayed there for seven years.

One night the light near the table goes out. As I was trying to screw in the bulb, I fell and hurt my wrist. I went to the Emergency Room, and they put my wrist in a splint. I headed back to my car. Suddenly, I could feel the presence of the Lord overtaking me. Somehow, I ended up at the lake. I began to pray.

My grandmother always told me if you don't know the words to pray, just talk to God. He will hear you. As I prayed out loud, the swans came to me. I jumped because I said what in the world! God, what is happening right now? No one would believe me about the swans gathering around me. Immediately, the Holy Ghost took over. Now, the swans listened as I spoke in my heavenly language.

I headed back to my car and immediately called BJ. He repeated what he originally said to me: ***"If I get to the lake, God is going to meet me there."*** I was so astonished by the vision I also called Regina to tell her about my experience. After I left Regina, I went to my car and headed home. Then I stayed in the house for the weekend.

A full vision comes over me, and everything opens. I saw a street of gold, and the gates were lit up. Then, I saw a big hand and heard a voice telling me to come to them. Once I enter the gates, they close behind me. I see a silhouette of a body. He tells me, "Once you get on this side, that's when I will ***receive.*** " When I left there, I beheld the vision and the vivid memory of it all.

It's Monday, and time to grind. I am in the Emergency Room setting up my EKG machine, ready to work. I was paged to the Emergency Room. I met a paramedic standing near my table. His name is Joe, and we started talking to each other. He wanted to know if I was going to the Respiratory Party. He stayed there until the X-ray was completed. I answered yes. But I don't have an escort. So, Joe took me to the party.

We get there and are seated at the table. We had one cup of wine. Suddenly, I felt like I was in a drunken state. Joe was completely turned off by it. Yet, God intervenes. Joe took me home.

The next day, Regina tells me why this happened to me. I agreed to go to the Watchnight service. She didn't want me to go on the motorcycle ride. Regina was one of the most persistent people I have ever met, trying to persuade me to go to church.

There was Bishop Smith from New York invited to minister. He started walking amongst the people in the congregation. All of this was new to me. He spoke to me, saying that I had been living a life in the world. After tonight, you will never go back again. I was slain in the Spirit. I received the Holy Spirit that night.

Slain in the Spirit.

There is an act known as being ***"slain in the Spirit."*** This occurs when a person is supposedly overcome by the power of the Holy Spirit and faints or falls to the ground in physical powerlessness.

John 18:6 says,

> *"As soon then as He had said unto them, I am He, they went backward and fell to the ground."*

Revelation 1:17 says,

> *"And when I saw Him, I fell at His feet as dead. And He laid His right hand upon me, saying unto me, Fear not; I am the first and the last:"*

Then, I started going to Bible Study with Regina. The Pastor asked if anyone had a testimony. I felt compelled to tell it. I shared my testimony about the vision. I couldn't believe the Pastor poked fun at me, asking, "If it happened on a big-screen TV." I was confused by it all.

When I got to work the next day, I saw my co-worker Kim and talked about it. Kim says, ***"Let's talk about it when you get time. I know you have been going to church with Regina. The Lord told me to tell you to come to church with me on Fridays for a five-a.m. prayer at Love and Unity with Pastor Ron Hill for three months."*** Okay, when I go there, the Pastor calls me out. Kim tells him she agreed to come to church with her. The Pastor asks me to tell my testimony about the streets of gold, the gate, and the crown. The Pastor then said, ***"God had a message for me about my vision."*** I felt like I was going crazy all over again.

This Pastor made me feel a sense of freedom, while the other Pastor made me feel like my testimony was a joke. I came to understand that people, babes in Christ, need understanding and guidance.

Pastor Ron Hill told me I was sold out for God. He started telling me about signs, wonders, and healing, giving me a better understanding. He told me the church I was going to was not mature enough to understand what I saw and was going through.

So, I stayed in a place of prayer. The Lord told me to 'hide Him in my heart.' From here, I learned to pray all day and night, seeking God's protection. The way to help myself was to pray without ceasing.

1 Thessalonians 5:16-18 says,

"Rejoice evermore. Pray without ceasing. In everything give thanks: for this is the will of the Father in Christ Jesus concerning you."

I want to take a moment to share with you my admiration for my grandmother. She was a truly remarkable woman of faith, who accomplished so much despite her limited education. In fact, she managed to purchase two houses and pay them off entirely, which is no small feat. She was also very dedicated to ensuring that her children would be taken care of and that they would receive their rightful inheritance.

I am grateful to have had such a strong and inspiring grandmother in my life, and I hope that her legacy continues to inspire others as well.

CHAPTER 2

GRANDMA STORIES

I can remember Grandma's stories like it was yesterday. She always shared her life with me. I remember her talking about being in Texas and how she picked cotton, lived with her grandma, and was not allowed to speak to people unless she was given the okay to talk. She told me about her being on the outside and the Lord would talk to her, which was where she began to hear the Lord's voice so very clearly.

She always talks about how her grandma would go into town for the Caucasian people to heal their family members, from husbands, wives, children, etc. My grandma said, ***"She could make medication from the plants, and she knew things by the weather she knew when Tornadoes were coming. When her son was coming into town, she could discern him coming."***

I thought this was such an amazing thing to hear from my grandmother. She said, ***"The Caucasian people blessed her for healing their family members and friends and that they gave her land and a house. They even named a street after her in Texas."*** My grandmother said, ***"She would be on the side of the house and the birds, and everything would come to her every morning."***

So, my great-grandmother went to California to set up a way to bring my grandmother and my great-uncle to the States. She started working for a very wealthy Jewish family, taking care of their home and as the nanny for their kids.

My great-grandmother was doing well. She opened up her own business, bought the property, and went back and got my grandmother and my great-uncle Frank into the States. My grandmother at that time was 12 years old. When I think of my grandma, who had eight kids and took care of them, she even had me most of the time. When she married Josh again, he bought her first home for her and the kids.

I remember growing up on Tarrant Street. My grandmother always helped people and gave them a place to live. I believe that's where I got that from helping people. Even when I got older, my grandma shared many stories about her life.

She shared a story about how she went to the Mental Hospital. She believed they were trying to kill her in there. "But the hand of God is on her life, and they couldn't touch her. She always reminded me of how God's hand is on me. My grandmother believed the Lord revealed how He protected me everywhere I go. She said, ***"I was never afraid of anything when I was a little girl. I would fight with the boys and win the fight. I always liked helping people and giving them things. I would even help the ones who didn't even like me."***

My grandmother, I have never seen someone with so much faith. She was a woman of great faith. Although she could not read well, she bought and paid for two houses. She's a woman who set up things for her kids so they would receive their inheritance. She taught me to listen to these things when somebody is talking because there is wisdom in it.

Don't get me wrong, my grandmother didn't make any mess even when her son David would bring people to the house. She would get them up out of there.

Today, when Listening to my grandmother talk about her life, I was deeply touched because she went through so much. We always think we go through so much until we hear someone else's story. She couldn't speak unless she was allowed to say anything. She had to play outside by herself and had no friends. I can't imagine how that was because I never had to experience that as a child.

I always had plenty of friends and plenty of family around me. So, I was quite spoiled even though my mother and father were not together. I spent time with both parents and both sides of the family, so I had an awesome childhood.

My grandmother is such a woman of great faith. When she prayed and saw the manifestation of signs, wonders, and miracles. I'm talking about rainbows coming into the house with colors that you can't even describe how pretty they are. I'm talking about supernatural money appearing in her purse. We both know that it wasn't there before so many miracles.

She has always prayed for me to have the best. I remember I told her I wanted my own house. She had me read scriptures in Psalm for seven days, and I would get approved to buy my house. I bought a nice family home. It was a three-bedroom, two-bath extended den in Long Beach. It was a beautiful home. I stayed there for five years.

God's Word on Wisdom

Wisdom is the principal thing. In getting wisdom, we must look upon our teachers as our fathers and grandparents: though instruction carries in it reproof and correction, bid it welcome in the teaching of wisdom.

Solomon was a man of wisdom. His parents loved him and therefore taught him. Wise and godly men, in every age of the world, and rank in society, agree that true wisdom consists in obedience, and is united to happiness.

An interest in Christ's salvation is necessary. This wisdom is the one thing needful. A soul without truth, wisdom and grace is a dead soul.

CHAPTER 3

FAITH THE WAY OF WISDOM

I could hear my grandmother praying and talking to God throughout the day and night. She truly believed in God, and no matter what, she was going to serve Him.

She turned around and said, ***"You must study the bible daily."*** My faith has given me wisdom. The Word of God gives us strength on the inside. Enough things are happening in this world that cause us to stay before Him. He is the answer.

Jeremiah 29:11 -13 says,

> *"For I know the thoughts that I think toward you, saith the LORD, thoughts of peace, and not of evil, to give you an expected end. ¹² Then shall ye call upon me, and ye shall go and pray unto me, and I will hearken unto you."*

Grandmother would get in her teaching moments where she wanted me to sit down and listen while she was cooking. She said, "Faith – You say to yourself, ***"I have faith in my friend."*** We have faith in people because they have proven themselves in the past, and expect them to do the same. But that's not faith. It's belief. **Belief is natural**. It requires evidence. **Faith is supernatural**. It does not mean we have faith in God because of anything He has done for us or we believe He will do. We have faith in God because of who He is, ***"He's God."***

I did learn from her that our faith grows through prayer and studying the Word of God. Some of the most difficult spots in my life have been made possible because of God. We gain more confidence when we understand the Word and walk in the revelation and wisdom of God. This is where we plug into the power source, which, by prayer, connects us to God. All of this is like learning math problems. The answer comes from configuring the process to learn how to solve the problem.

Godly wisdom is described in **Psalm 111:10,**

> *"The fear of the Lord is the beginning of wisdom; a good understanding has all those who do His commandments."*

Human wisdom is described in **Proverbs 14:12-13,**

> *"There is a way which seemeth right unto a man, but the end thereof is the ways of death. [13] Even in laughter the heart is sorrowful, and the end of that mirth is heaviness."*

According to God's inspired word, wisdom isn't a matter of analyzing things and arriving at your conclusion. You need to understand that you have the wisdom to realize that He is the Creator of the entire universe and He's on your side.

"Four classes of wisdom, according to **James 3:** *earthly wisdom, intellectual wisdom, devilish wisdom and the wisdom from above.*

James 3:15-17 (KJV) *"This wisdom descendeth not from above, but is earthly, sensual, devilish. [16] For where envying and strife is, there is confusion and every evil work. [17] But the wisdom that is from above is first pure, then peaceable, gentle, and easy to be intreated, full of mercy and good fruits, without partiality, and without hypocrisy."*

James 1:5-6 says,

"If any of you lack <u>wisdom</u>, let him ask of God, that giveth to all men liberally, and upbraideth not; and it shall be given him. [6] But let him ask in <u>faith</u>, nothing wavering. For he that watereth is like a wave of the sea driven with the wind and tossed."

Don't let anyone fool you into balancing your faith and wisdom. Your *faith* is *wisdom*. Nothing is wiser than relying on your Creator as you follow Him and His unending love for you. Through **faith** and **wisdom**, we are releasing the mind of God when we pray and confess His Word.

We must have the *wisdom* to know nothing is impossible for those who believe. Our *faith* is the key to seeing miracles and breakthroughs consistently.

Learning how to plug into the power source of God, the Holy Spirit, in the Word of God, builds us in faith. We experience greater confidence when we understand the Word and walk in the Revelation and wisdom of God.

It plugs us into the power source, and prayer connects us to God. He will show us great and mighty things! We have to operate in God's wisdom to defeat the power of the enemy. We must know we walk into the Authority of God.

The Word of God is the SWORD OF THE SPIRIT.

Ephesian 6:17 says,

"And take the helmet of salvation, and the sword of the Spirit, which is the Word."

I could hear my grandmother praying and talking to God throughout the day. She truly believed in God, and no matter what, she was going to serve Him.

She turned around and said, ***"You must study the bible daily. My faith has given me wisdom."***

Romans 10:16-18 says,

> *"But they have not all obeyed the gospel. For Esaias saith, Lord, who hath believed our report? [17] So then faith cometh by hearing and hearing by the word of God.[18] But I say, Have they not heard? Yes verily, their sound went into all the earth, and their words unto the ends of the world."*

Are you one who has not obeyed the gospel? Where is your faith? *"Faith comes by hearing and hearing the Word of God"* **(Romans 10:17)**, for faith is standing on God's Word. If you don't know God's Word, you cannot stand on God's Word. The more of the Word of God you hear, the more of His Word you can stand on.

What, then, is faith? Faith is a spiritual concept. It is made very clear in **Hebrews 11:1** Amplified Bible; *"Now faith is the assurance* (title deed, confirmation) *of things hoped for (divinely guaranteed), and the evidence of things not seen [the conviction of their reality—faith comprehends as fact what cannot be experienced by the physical senses]."*

The will decides to act on what the mind believes is true. The mind reads something in Scripture, and in our spirit, the Holy Spirit says, **'Yes, that's true,' and we say, 'Yes, that's true,'** and then in our will we make a choice to step out in that truth. That step is faith.

There is no power in faith itself. The power is found in the object of faith: Jesus Christ." May Jesus be the object of your faith today and every day, and may you share the good news about Him as often as possible.

Faith in Action is seen when God's people allow their belief/faith in God's Word to move them to action. If we begin to act in ways that demonstrate belief. Then, we can walk in God's authority.

The ***Word of God*** is our source of wisdom. We must operate in God's wisdom to defeat the power of the enemy; understanding the Revelation of wisdom is the key to authority.

Man's wisdom, by contrast, is notoriously frail and fallible. We are easily perplexed by the rudimentary difficulties of everyday life. We desperately need wisdom, and we often find it elusive.

As God's Children, We Need Wisdom.

Scripture reminds us that God is the source of all True Wisdom. For *"The reverent and worshipful fear of the Lord is the beginning (the chief and choice part) of Wisdom, and the knowledge of the Holy One is insight and understanding"* (**Proverbs 9:10** Amplified Bible, Classic Edition). In other words, our need for wisdom ought to motivate us to turn to God—and those who refuse to turn to God have no hope of ever being truly wise.

Peter received the kingdom's keys after receiving the revelation that Jesus was Christ. Let us see what Jesus tells His disciples, Peter, and we, the church of today.

Core Issue of Discipleship

Let's look at **Matthew 16:19** in the Amplified Bible, Classic Edition

> *"I will give you the keys of the kingdom of heaven; and whatever you bind (declare to be improper and unlawful) on earth [a]must be what is already bound in heaven; and whatever you loose (declare lawful) on earth [b]must be what is already loosed in heaven."*

How we understand **Spiritual Authority** and the **Power of Faith** is found in,

Luke **10:10-20,**

> *"But into whatsoever city ye enter, and they receive you not, go your ways out into the streets of the same, and say, [11] Even the very dust of your city, which cleaveth on us, we do wipe off against you: notwithstanding be ye sure of this, that the kingdom of God is come nigh unto you. [12] But I say unto you, that it shall be more tolerable in that day for Sodom, than for that city. [13] Woe unto thee, Chorazin! woe unto thee, Bethsaida! for if the mighty works had been done in Tyre and Sidon, which have been done in you, they had a great while ago repented, sitting in sackcloth and ashes. [14] But it shall be more tolerable for Tyre and Sidon at the judgment, than for you. [15] And thou, Capernaum, which art exalted to heaven, shalt be thrust down to hell. [16] He that heareth you*

heareth me; and he that despiseth you despiseth me; and he that despiseth me despiseth him that sent me. ¹⁷ And the seventy returned again with joy, saying, Lord, even the devils are subject unto us through thy name. ¹⁸ And he said unto them, I beheld Satan as lightning fall from heaven. ¹⁹ Behold, I give unto you power to tread on serpents and scorpions, and over all the power of the enemy: and nothing shall by any means hurt you. ²⁰ Notwithstanding in this rejoice not, that the spirits are subject unto you; but rather rejoice, because your names are written in heaven."

We need to understand that **ALL power & and authority come from God.**

Romans 13:1 says,

*"**Let every soul** be subject unto the higher powers. For there is no power but of God: the powers that be are ordained of God. ² Whosoever therefore resisteth the power, resisteth the ordinance of God: and they that resist shall receive to themselves damnation."*

"For there is no power but of God." All power and authority come from God. For every person in government, either elected or appointed, even if they are part of a monarchy and born into power, all the authority they have comes from God. The boss at work, mom and dad, teachers at school, a coach, even the pimply-faced kid with "shift leader" on his name tag at the burger joint, all of them have some sort of authority, some more than others, but everyone has received their power from God. God is the ultimate authority.

In **Matthew 16:13-19,**

> *"When Jesus came into the coasts of Caesarea Philippi, he asked his disciples, saying, Whom do men say that I the Son of man am? [14] And they said, Some say that thou art John the Baptist: some, Elias; and others, Jeremias, or one of the prophets.[15] He saith unto them, But whom say ye that I am? [16] And Simon Peter answered and said, Thou art the Christ, the Son of the living God. [17] And Jesus answered and said unto him, Blessed art thou, Simon Barjona: for flesh and blood hath not revealed it unto thee, but my Father which is in heaven. [18] And I say also unto thee, That thou art Peter, and upon this rock I will build my church; and the gates of hell shall not prevail against it. [19] And I will give unto thee the keys of the kingdom of heaven: and whatsoever thou shalt bind on earth shall be bound in heaven: and whatsoever thou shalt loose on earth shall be loosed in heaven."*

Jesus posed certain questions to Peter: Who do you think I am? What did God say? He gave Peter keys to operate and use them by faith and with wisdom, understanding that we have been given the Legal right to use the name of Jesus. We receive power through the Holy Spirit. **Acts 1:8** says,

> *"But ye shall receive power, after that the Holy Ghost is come upon you: and ye shall be witnesses unto me both in Jerusalem, and in all Judaea, and in Samaria, and unto the uttermost part of the earth."*

We're living in a fallen world, so we will always be tempted by sin. So, as believers in Jesus, we need to take time to understand the battle between the flesh and the Spirit; so that we can learn how important it is to be walking in the leading of the Spirit.

Look, We're in a Spiritual Warfare. Satan hates us and wants to destroy us. We must be aware of the devil's devices, weapons, and tactics because our spiritual life depends on them.

Ephesians 4:14-15 says,

"That we henceforth be no more children, tossed to and fro, and carried about with every wind of doctrine, by the sleight of men, and cunning craftiness, whereby they lie in wait to deceive; ¹⁵ But speaking the truth in love, may grow up into Him in all things, which is the head, even Christ:"

The greatest generals are great statisticians and strategists; without WISDOM, you cannot win without a strategy. We lose, but God's Word already told us that we have the victory.

1 Corinthians 15:57 says,

"But thanks be to God, which giveth us the victory through our Lord Jesus Christ."

We understand that David's victories prepared the way for his son, Solomon, a wise man who enjoyed peace and prosperity.

David was a king who understood the place of prayer.

The prayer of David ended with him praying that the Glory of the Lord filled the land.

Psalm 72:18-20 says,

"18 Blessed be the LORD God, the God of Israel, who only doeth wondrous things. 19 And blessed be his glorious name for ever: and let the whole earth be filled with His glory; Amen, and Amen. 20 The prayers of David the son of Jesse are ended."

David prayed that the whole earth would be filled with God's glory.

Habakkuk 2:14 says,

"For the earth shall be filled with the knowledge of the glory of the Lord, as the waters cover the sea."

Habakkuk 2:14 is a promise to you and me. Let me say it again. *The Earth will be filled with the knowledge of the glory of the Lord as the waters cover the sea.*

Amidst all the challenges in this world today, that you and I are walking through, that the people of God are experiencing at this moment in time, this promise breaks through. It's like a sunrise in the east. With the light coming over the horizon, we are reminded that one day these trials shall pass. That one day, these difficulties will be no more for the people of God, for all who trust in God. As Christians, we have confidence that a day is coming when the knowledge of the glory of the Lord will cover the earth as the waters cover the sea.

There is coming a day when His glory will fill the Earth. The knowledge of His glory and enjoyment of His glory are like waters covering the sea. This is what Jesus taught us to pray for, your kingdom comes, you will be done on Earth as it is in heaven, and it's going to happen one day.

So, continue to pray without ceasing. God is the source of our wisdom and strategies. His Word is the source of our understanding. WISDOM is the principal thing.

Proverbs 4:7-9, says,

"Wisdom is the principal thing; therefore get wisdom: and with all thy getting get understanding. 8 Exalt her, and she shall promote thee: she shall bring thee to honour, when thou dost embrace her. 9 She shall give to thine head an ornament of grace: a crown of glory shall she deliver to thee."

My Great-Grandma always talked to me about *WISDOM*. She said, ***"Always be a lady. When you give your life to Christ, always be a woman of God with integrity, good characteristics, honesty, faithful, loyal, and truth".*** That' grandma *WISDOM*.

Do you get it? We will have wisdom if we align our life with the Principles of God.

All you have to do is ask for *WISDOM,* which you will receive. Ask God for wisdom. I did and I received it with faith and believe that nothing is too hard for God.

Daniel continued in prayer even though the King ordered him not to pray. He was found on his knees praying by two strangers who told the King. Praying at all costs is a serious matter. Just believe Jesus gave us the power to tread over serpents and scorpions.

Matthew 10:1 says,

"And when He had called unto Him His twelve disciples, He gave them power against unclean spirits, to cast them out, and to heal all manner of sickness and all manner of disease."

Luke 10:19 says,

"Behold, I give unto you the power to tread on serpents and scorpions, and over all the power of the enemy: and nothing shall by any means hurt you."

He Promises *"that nothing will by any means harm us."* Some believers fear engagement. They are afraid of backlash. Jesus sent his disciples out to engage the enemy. they were told to heal the sick and to cast out devils. We have to combine the power of the Holy Spirit with the authority of the name of Jesus to route the enemy.

Make sure your sins are forgiven. **Do not engage the enemy without confessing (own upto your sin) sin in your life.** There is power in the Blood of Jesus.

We see in **1 John 1:9,**

"If we confess our sins, he is faithful and just to forgive us our sins, and to cleanse us from all unrighteousness."

Our Heavenly Father loves to bless His obedient children. He moves out ahead of us, He sends people to you to bless you, as He's preparing the way for us, and always supplies our every need (**Note:** He supplies all our needs, not some of our needs) as we follow Him in faith and love. He doesn't promise a lack of trials.

Philippians 4:19 lets us know,

*"But my God **shall supply** all your need according to his riches in glory by Christ Jesus."*

"Shall supply" is a promise that was given to a church that had sacrificially given to meet Paul's need. **Your need** made it clear that Paul was concerned about not only his own situation but also that of the Philippians. Paul assured them that God has more than enough to cover their need: **his riches in glory by Christ Jesus** sets forth the measure of God's supply (see Eph. 1:18; 3:16-20).

We are to continue to shout our praise even when we're hemmed in with troubles. We need to understand that our presence of praise is voiced continually in heaven since **Deuteronomy 20:4** lets us know that *the LORD your God is the one who goes with you to fight for you against your enemies to give you victory."* In that case, our voices should always be lifted up in praise of our Lord.

We are told in **1 Thessalonians 5:16-18,**

"Rejoice evermore. Pray without ceasing. In everything give thanks: for this is the will of God in Christ Jesus concerning you."

Our Lord God tells us here that we are to have an attitude of joy, thanksgiving, and prayer at all times, no matter the conditions or circumstances surrounding us. He's not telling us (He's commanding us) that we are to thank God for bad things and tragedies that come our way. It means staying joyful no matter what is happening in our lives because we have the Lord, and in Him, we shall overcome no matter what the devil is trying to do to us.

He doesn't want us to thank Him for the bad things that happen but thank Him that we have victory in all things in Christ.

We are not to become bitter over life's circumstances but rather to continue to rejoice in the Lord. It is the will of God for us to rejoice no matter what comes. It is not the will of God to receive evil things from Him. It is an insult to God to thank Him for accidents, sickness, tragedy, etc. He does not send those things to us; the devil does. We're told to resist the devil and submit to God.

We are told in **James 4:7,**

> *"Submit yourselves therefore to God. Resist the devil, and he will flee from you."*

We are to love and rejoice in the Lord despite what the devil tries to do to us. We know how troubles can develop passionate patience in us and how that patience, in turn, forges the tempered steel of virtue, keeping us alert for whatever God will do next. In alert expectancy such as this, we're never left feeling shortchanged. Quite the contrary—we can't round up enough containers to hold everything God generously pours into our lives through the Holy Spirit. **He does promise eventual victory.**

Jeremiah 17:7-8 says,

> *"Blessed is the man that trusteth in the Lord, and whose hope the Lord is. ⁸ For he shall be as a tree planted by the waters, and that spreadeth out her roots by the river, and shall not see when heat cometh, but her leaf shall be green; and shall not be careful in the year of drought, neither shall cease from yielding fruit."*

Nothing paralyzes our lives like the attitude that things can never change. We need to remind ourselves that God can change things. Outlook determines the outcome. If we see only the problems, we will be defeated, but if we see the possibilities in the problems, we can have victory. - Warren Wiersbe

Psalm 116:8-12

" For thou hast delivered my soul from death, mine eyes from tears, and my feet from falling. ⁹ I will walk before the LORD in the land of the living.¹⁰ I believed, therefore have I spoken: I was greatly afflicted:¹¹ I said in my haste, All men are liars.¹² What shall I render unto the LORD for all his benefits toward me?"

CHAPTER 4

PRAYER SAVED MY LIFE

It was the middle of the night, and I awakened suddenly. I was carrying on a conversation with God. Most nights, I would cry out to the Lord about what happened during the day, or I wanted clarity emotionally moving forward. So, I fluffed up my pillows as if someone else was lying beside me. I said, *"Lord, everybody else tells me who I am, but whom do you say I am?"* I know I believe in the Word of God by faith. It is the essence of life and a daily process as I study God's Word. So many things have happened as a little girl, showing me how to stand firm. My Great Grandmother always prayed for me and my ways of life. Here I am now as a young woman trying to find my Purpose. She stepped in and told me to pray during troubled times, especially because we are fighting the devil. Somebody could have killed me. I can make it if I have a prayer life.

At the time, I was with my friend Al, and we were in the car, 'skinning and grinning' and getting to know one another. I thought our friendship would be the start of something new and different. He treated me with such kindness in the beginning. He pulled over to a gas station so I could buy some cigarettes. I went inside the store, and when I came back out, these men pulled their guns on me. I raised my hands and said, *"What is going on?"* Al never exited the car, saying, *"Get in the car. Let's go."* I jumped inside that automobile. He took off. I said, *"Okay, but let me lead you because if you don't know where you are going, you'll end up on a dead-end street."*

So, once he turned down this street, it was a dead-end, and Al froze and just stopped. I yelled, ***"Oh my God."*** The car rode up behind us and let loose on our vehicle. I ducked down on the floor of the car.

The men came even closer and continued shooting at the vehicle. I said to myself this is it! I thought I was going to die. I pleaded with God, ***"Please do not let me die like this."*** I believed God before I knew Him in this circumstance. I was counting on God to stand in the gap for me. Honestly, the only prayer I ever knew was the Lord's Prayer. I called out the prayer frantically to help me in this hour. It may not have been the right way to pray but as long as I communicated with God, I was heard.

When the shooting stopped, I started praising God because the men drove away, and neither of us was hurt. Al was a big-time drug dealer. He got up and checked to see if we were okay. He did not try to explain. I never knew the truth about what happened that night. `

I was wrong again.

We went back to my aunt's house together. Everybody would have believed I set him up if I had returned without him, and he was dead. We didn't talk at all after what happened that night. I am still shaking the dust off and looking all around me.

I told the Lord, ***"All jokes aside, but if you are trying to get my attention, I am listening."*** I laid before the Lord weeping. I could still hear my Great-Grandmother praying the Words of the Bible.

The Lord protected me through my great-grandmother until she died. I jumped up, looked under my bed, grabbed the Bible, and held it close to my bosom. I felt safe in the arms of Jesus. I thank you, Lord, for my life. In my heart, I do honor you.

When a man or woman truly loves God, every fiber of their being surrenders unto Him. It is demonstrated in our trust. Jesus calls for us to let our emotions, attitudes, and convictions express our love toward Him.

As the tears began to stream down my face, I said, ***"Here I am, Lord. I give myself to you."*** I continued reciting the Lord's Prayer with my arms outstretched. I could feel the presence of God in the room.

Surrendering to God is hard when it is not daily. My prayer daily is to surrender to God, His will, His way, every day in a fresh way.

It's like the world was at peace. I knew God was calling me to realize I am His daughter. I knew the pain of my past relationships had to cease.

I learned all abusive relationships involve an imbalance of power. My abusive relationships dealt with men who intimidated and threatened violence, hitting, slapping, and beating me. **I had to choose how I wanted to live my life.** I started reading the Word of God.

Matthew 22:37 says,

"Jesus said unto him, and thou shalt love the Lord thy God with all thy heart, and with all thy soul, and with all thy mind."

Before we go on, let us understand the word 'love' that Jesus is talking about. What He's talking about isn't born just out of emotions, feelings, familiarity, or attraction. This love comes from the will and is a choice; it requires faithfulness, commitment, and sacrifice without ever expecting anything in return. It is a Greek word pronounced ah-gah-pay, better known as Agape. Jesus is talking about Agapa Love.

My life started to change that night. I would be a woman after God's own heart. There was no other way to live without God in my life. All God wanted from me was to live for Him. The kind of Love God showed me meant a man could not satisfy the longing in my heart. As I began to seek God daily, He drew me closer to Him. The soul hurts were deeply embedded. I needed God in my life/

Men deceived me in almost every way. The men claiming to love me had fleshly attractions. They would give me money, cars, clothes, and jewelry. Then, they chose to beat me. **We were partakers in domestic violence.** They didn't love me unconditionally. I was a cover for what they were doing. If it looked like we were an honest couple, it met the man's needs. The only exception is that he did not want me to think 'on my own.' The men had motives with me as an armpiece to hide their ring of stolen cars and selling drugs.

I was to be seen and not heard. The men wanted to maintain power in the relationship. Only God receives our broken hearts and puts us back together again.

Acts 20:24 says,

"But none of these things move me, neither count my life dear unto myself, so that I might finish my course with joy, and the ministry I have received of the Lord Jesus, to testify the gospel of the grace of God."

I later learned they were seducing spirits and deceptive attachments. The men gave me money, cars, clothes, and jewelry but chose domestic violence out of jealousy. You cannot crucify true Love. Life looked normal through the eyes of the onlookers. My life would have to be changed if I were to live.

1 Timothy 4:1 says,

"Now the Spirit speaketh expressly, that in the latter times, some shall depart from the faith, giving heed to seducing spirits, and doctrines of devils;"

Introspectively, the enemy roared through my life, trying to take me out. In many cases, I feared for my life. These men wanted to own me, and if I denied them, they beat me. Many abusers learn violence from their families and repeat the toxic patterns. How many pounds of flesh would it take to realize I needed to walk away? I needed to understand that these men were victimizing me fully. They threatened, coerced, and intimidated me with guns and pummeled me with their hands. The sex was never consensual because I knew he might get angry if I did not do it.

They told me I belonged to them and better do what they say. Sometimes, it turned into both of us hitting each other. So anyway, they could gain control was used by them. The men knew what kind of lifestyle I was used to having. So, instead of giving me money, they made me ask for it.

It was fact over fiction.

God shows us our weakness so we can see that it is by His grace and mercy that we have the power to do these things. We need to open up to God. If the men apologized that was enough. One even told me I made him so angry he had to beat me. So, I prayed daily for deliverance.

Psalms 34:16-17; 22 says,

> *"The face of the Lord is against them that do evil, to cut the remembrance of them from the earth. The righteous cry and the Lord heareth, and deliverth them from all their troubles. The Lord redeemeth the soul of His servants and none of them that trust in Him shall be desolate."*

The Word of the Lord let me know that I would be all right. The Lord is near those who have broken hearts. All of the evil things that happened to me through violence shall be cut off. Most of the men who beat me ended up in prison on major charges against them for drugs and stolen cars.

Did any of the people around me know that I was emotionally shattered?

After every incident, I felt so much pain on the inside. I developed a nervous tick and shook all over my body.

Abuse is learned, and how you enter the relationship determines the choice to survive or get out immediately.

I would always look to see if my son was sleeping. I never wanted my son to see me hurt. So, I would put my face in my pillow and cry.

Psalm 56:8 Living Bible (TLB) says

"You have seen me tossing and turning through the night. You have collected all my tears and preserved them in your bottle! You have recorded every one in your book."

Sometimes, I cry because life's sorrows have become chronic, filling my life like these unwelcome men that God Himself allowed to come into my life. Other times, I cry because some unexpected misery lands like a meteor and carves a crater in my soul. And still, other times, I cry and don't quite know why.

As I cry into my pillow, God let me know through His Word that He collects my tears in bottles.

Now I understand; it might seem God couldn't possibly care about me or my situation. Sometimes, it might feel like I am alone in this world, and so many things seem to be going wrong. I end up crying and crying and wondering if God even cares about me.

My friends, during my lifetime, I have learned that God cares more for me than anyone on this whole earth could ever care, and He sees all my tears. The bible tells you and me that He collects them in a bottle. He knows what we're going through; if you could just look at Him through His Word, it would confirm that for us. He cares so much about us. He knows every thought we have, every ache we have in our hearts, and all our desires.

I understand more now what God is telling me in **Psalm 56: 8**; *"He has collected all my tears in His bottle and has recorded each one in his book."* That shows me that not only does God know every single tear that I've cried but He keeps track of what made me cry and He studies my heartbreak so that He can heal my comfort and give (He has) me joy in a way that is unique to only me.

James 4:7 says,

"Submit yourselves, then, to God. Resist the devil, and he will flee from you. So, humble yourselves before God. Resist the devil, and he will flee from you."

There are several essential things to consider. If any glimmer of your light shines without reinforcements, it's a target for the enemy to attack you. We need to know our abuser, what it looks like, how it talks to us, and how it makes us feel. **Ask yourself, "Do I feel isolated from other people and family or like I did something to cause a situation.?** Am I submitting to God or man? I had conflicting messages in my mind for a minute. If I resisted them, they would sometimes beat me even worse. We must understand the power of faith.

If I truly believed God by faith, He would deliver me from all evil.

Apostle Paul teaches us in **Ephesians 6:10,**

"Finally, be strong in the Lord and in the power of His might."

Deceit was the ultimate aim.

The devil wanted to get you sidetracked and confused in your mindset to ambush you in the Spirit. It is emotional for men and all about the rush and sudden assault. The longer I stay before the Lord, the stronger I become. The enemy doesn't have staying power if I am continuously seeking God.

I say to myself every morning before I start my day:

"I AM MORE THAN A CONQUEROR"

It's funny that as a little girl, I learned to rejoice with thanksgiving no matter how small or great my success. When I was paralyzed, I talked to God about my healing and believed a miracle would come. When I could move my legs, then stand up on my legs and walk across the room, we all gave God the glory for what He had done.

As a teenager, I witnessed the power of full-fledged faith and divine healing. The doctors said, ***"I might never walk again."*** It's not over until God says it's over. `I could hear the Lord saying the words of **Colossians 3:12** telling me,

> *"So, as those who have been chosen of God, holy and beloved, put on a heart of compassion, kindness, humility, gentleness, and patience."*

I learned to fight my battles on my knees and pray the Word. The sum of all my experiences made me surrender to Jesus Christ. God told me in 2022," This was the year of the Armor, for the enemy comes to hurt your soul. I wanted to be free. *' Be ye not deceived, for God is not mocked."* God had to deliver me from the mindset of daring somebody to mess with me so I could kill them.

So, I could shoot. I was packing. My gun was in my purse. Never will I be in the old situation of being battered and abused by men with no identity.

God's Word is light.

It is the trick of the enemy to destroy your character.

I had to put on my war clothes embodied in the likeness of God: Love, peace, joy, and righteousness required me to live with integrity and be a witness to Him. The way to victory over the flesh is thus "living, walking, being led by the Spirit." Our mission is to grow in grace.

You Have an Adversary – All, not some things, but! ALL THINGS are possible through Jesus, you do, have an adversary who *"walks around like a roaring lion, seeking whom he may devour"* (1 Peter 5:8). Being more than a conqueror in Christ means that you have the power to resist him and stand firm in the faith. By faith *"I Am More Than A Conqueror"*

2 Peter 3:18 says,

"But grow in grace and the knowledge of our Lord and Saviour Jesus Christ. To him be glory both now and forever. Amen. "

WE ARE TO GROW IN GRACE, AND THE PROVISION OF GRACE MOVES ON IN US.

Our lives imparted by grace must be sustained by grace. This is a part of our freedom from strongholds and workers of iniquity. Grace is a continual thing. We must be sanctified by grace.

1- Look at how we stand in grace: Romans 5:2 (NLT) says,

> *"Because of our faith, Christ has brought us into this place of undeserved privilege where we now stand, and we confidently and joyfully look forward to sharing God's glory."*

2- In rough times, God proves that His Grace is sufficient. Ephesians 1:7 says,

> *"By whom also we have access by faith into this grace wherein we stand, and rejoice in hope of the glory of God."*

WE MUST BE TAUGHT TO BE STRENGTHENED AND HAVE HOPE IN JESUS.

3- In Christ, you are gracefully broken. Here, we are taught, trained, and disciplined by grace. 1 Titus 2:11-14 says,

> *"For the grace of God that bringeth salvation hath appeared to all men, [12]Teaching us that, denying ungodliness and worldly lusts, we should live soberly, righteously, and godly, in this present world; [13] Looking for that blessed hope, and the glorious appearing of the great God and our Saviour Jesus Christ; [14] Who gave himself for us, that he might redeem us from all iniquity, and purify unto himself a peculiar people, zealous of good works."*

4- The true question becomes, *"Do I want to be free?"*

God has given the Word of God to develop you.

We cannot be deceived at this hour. God's Word is life. We must know how the devil is coming to taunt us. The devil has his tactics and snares.

Think about this: The Prophet Samuel was looking for David. He was looking for the one. Like the enemy, he searched for the next King with all his tactics. We have to look for the intent in people.

God will allow us to discern the enemy in the spirit.

The Prophet did not stop until he finished his assignment. The enemy wants to find his next one. We must remember we are not dealing with natural bets on our lives.

The devil has bullets and a gun too.

To maintain my stance, I had to labor in prayer for victory. Once I put on my Armor, God gave me victory. He prepared the way—the peace that I needed I could not obtain through a man. As we say

sometimes, he was a good lover, but what about? My body, mind, or beauty? God regenerates us to experience His love, joy, and peace.

He will lead me correctly if I seek the Lord's guidance and direction.

John 14:27 says,

"Peace I leave with you, my peace I give unto you: not as the world giveth, give I unto you. Let not your heart be troubled, neither let it be afraid."

Domestic Violence Quotes on Surviving

"You are not the darkness you endured. You are the light that refused to surrender."

John Mark Green

CHAPTER 5

DOMESTIC VIOLENCE

Psalms 35:4 says,

"Let them be confounded and put to shame that seek after my soul: let them be turned back and brought to confusion that devise my hurt."

I prayed for my way out of bad relationships. Specifically, the violence I experienced was a pattern in my life. The men I was involved with wanted to control every aspect of my life, including domestic violence.

I was being battered and abused by men who said they loved me. I was living in darkness. It became a soul tie (sexual relationship) and a stronghold (bound). I allowed myself to feel unworthy, guilty, and ashamed. I continued to pray to God for help to show me the way.

Domestic violence, domestic abuse, and intimate partner violence, it's a pattern of behavior in a relationship that is used to gain or maintain power and control when there is a close relationship between the offender and the victim. It's not necessarily the bruises on the body that hurt. It's the wounds of the heart and the scars on the mind that creates a soul hurt and every soul hurt tells a story

Each individual is responsible for themselves. I had to work on my relationship with God. This is personal to me. I asked how I could know God without having a real prayer life. Essentially, prayer is how we communicate with God. I chose to live according to God's Word and not man's.

Domestic violence is a pattern of abusive behavior in any relationship that one partner uses to gain or maintain control over another intimate partner. I needed to acknowledge what was happening to me by the men in my life. Most certainly, physical or psychological violence can affect anyone. It starts with small words and gestures, tracing your steps, questioning your whereabouts, and staring at you silently. I was threatened and called names, leaving me wondering what was going to happen next. It affects me even now.

Some women suffer from anxiety, depression, trauma, Post Traumatic Stress Disorder (PTSD). When we pray specifically to God, changes will happen because we believe and have faith. Once the men were in prison, I was able to walk away and get help. I realized that I was so angry inside.

I told the doctor that my face and left jaw would swell up in stressful situations. The doctor explained that every symptom originates in the body's response to the original trauma, which is called a physiological connection. One can develop chronic vigilance and sensitivity. The question becomes, how do we learn to trust ourselves or anyone else?

I keep telling the doctor *I am not a victim. I am a victor.* I realize there will be memories and triggers from time to time, but for my sake, I choose to move on. I had to understand what deliverance looked like!

The only physician I ever spoke to was God, the Great Physician. **My deliverance is tied up in my choices.** God gives us free will. You cannot move forward with chaos all around.

The Word of the Lord says in **Psalm 37: 8-9** says,

"Cease from anger and forsake wrath; Do not fret---it only causes harm. For evildoers shall be cut off, But those who wait on the Lord, They shall inherit the earth."

Some men beat, stomped, or pistol-whipped their women, and one rammed a gun in the throat. I was seriously injured and hospitalized as a result of it when one man busted my lip fully and I had to have surgery. I hid my face on the left side, hoping no one saw my injuries.

In a few sessions, the doctor informed me that domestic violence has long or short-term consequences, which can be psychological and physical.

'Your body keeps the score.'

It is almost like the law; a person can serve time for every act or touch to harm another's body. Then the body remembers, and you want to forget. I remember one true thing about God: He is a preserver. He can make me whole again. He is Jehovah Rapha, my healer. The Lord is the God of the Mountain and the God of Sheol.

When I lay before the Lord, basking in His presence, God knows who I am.

If you are in an abusive situation, you might recognize this pattern: you are threatened, the more abusive strikes, they apologize, promise to change, and offer gifts, and the cycle repeats itself. So, **it is crucial that we recognize and acknowledge the abuse and then break the cycle.**

I have learned that men will see your light. They can tell where a person's heart is based on what they do.

I told the doctor I was stalked, raped, shot at, and physically abused. For a few years, every man started with good intentions trying to meet my expectations. I began to look inward at the things that happened to me to see if I had a revelation for the people.

To begin healing, I started a group allowing other women to talk about relationships in a safe, non-judgmental environment. My group is called **Heart 2 Heart**.

I took action to acknowledge I was no longer interested in the relationship. I felt protected by my family, who embraced me wholeheartedly. We have to consider the fact that the problem in some cases is there are people in our life who couldn't understand our trauma or their own.

The longer you stay in it, the more emotional toll. Amid adversity, bind all confusion, soul-ties, and strongholds (devil). God is our stronghold in a strong city. Let Him direct your path. Pray the Word of God daily over your mind, heart, and body.

Psalm 62:5-8 says,

"My soul, wait thou only upon God; for my expectation is from Him.[6] He only is my rock and my salvation: he is my defence; I shall not be moved. [7] In God is my salvation and my glory: the rock of my strength, and my refuge, is in God [8] Trust in Him at all times; ye people, pour out your heart before Him: God is a refuge for us. Selah."

What I had to understand was how to help myself. To facilitate self-care, I needed total deliverance. My soul cried out to the Lord daily. When I understood I could share with the women in the group.

We must examine ourselves by looking deeper in our soul. I could no longer seek companionship and be called 'golden eyes' by a man when I was the apple of God's eyes.'

These relationships were like the song, *'Love on a two-way street.'* Whose Report do we believe? Most of the relationships had seducing spirits and deceptive attachments. I had to come clean with God about everything. You can't declare healing or anything if it is not based on God's Word, which delivers the truth and His righteousness.

Believe it or not, we are in a transition:

People, patterns, and things

Do we realize all of our help comes from the Lord? When God's presence moved, faith was moved out of our sight. Since we can't make order out of someone else's chaos, we have to leave and let the dead things die. **We will begin to shift because God is moving us.**

GOD is my everything. He is the Great Physician. Finally, I have found the strength in Him to tell my story. **For real change to occur, the body needs to know the danger has passed, and now I live in God's reality.**

Quotes by Charles Spurgeon

"And if the old gospel is not competent to work a revival, then we will do without the revival. Revival begins by Christians getting right first and then spills over into the world. If we want revivals, we must revive our reverence for the Word of God."

CHAPTER 6

THE SEASON OF REVERSAL

The Season of Reversal happens when God reverses every hostile, destructive, broken, shameful condition in your life. If you want to see changes happen in your life, you've got to get a vision that goes beyond what you've already seen and experienced. One leader said, 'An excellent place to look for that vision is the promises contained in God's promises found in the Word of God.

Isaiah 42:9 (Complete Jewish Bible) says,

"See how the former predictions come true, and now I declare new things before they sprout, I tell you about them."

As we understand God's ways, we can speak His truth. I believe God can do all things, and there is justice. God will encourage the bruised and hurt both physically and spiritually. Chances will shift us, but He serves us daily through constant love, care, guidance, and intercession. God prays over us daily.

He sings over us. **Zephaniah 3:17** says,

"The Lord your God in your midst, The mighty one, will save, he will rejoice over you with gladness, he will quiet you with love, he will rejoice over you with singing."

More intimately, I know that God has called me. The experiences that I went through don't make me damaged goods or anyone else. I have gained strength every day walking with the Lord. The Lord told me as He told the crippled man in John 5:8, *".Rise, take up thy bed, and walk."*

John 5:6-9 says,

"When Jesus saw him lie, and knew that he had been now a long time in that case, He saith unto him, Wilt thou be made whole? [7] The impotent man answered him, Sir, I have no man, when the water is troubled, to put me into the pool: but while I am coming, another steppeth down before me. [8] Jesus saith unto him, Rise, take up thy bed, and walk. [9] And immediately the man was made whole, and took up his bed, and walked: and on the same day was the sabbath."

This man did not even know anything about Jesus. But this man's faith in the desire to be healed and in his obedience to Jesus' (the Word of God) command.

John 5:12-13 says,

Then asked they him, What man is that which said unto thee, Take up thy bed, and walk? [13] And he that was healed wist not who it was: for Jesus had conveyed himself away, a multitude being in that place.

For at the logos (reality/true) Word of Jesus, he attempted to do what on so many occasions he had surely tried and failed to do at the moving of the water: *"Rise."* The man *"was made whole,"* not only sound but also robust. No physical therapy on his muscles and limbs, for when Jesus heals, it's complete. The man was the proof that Jesus was the healer. Like the man at the Pool of Bethesda (the sheep market pool)

Even though I may not have known about the Savior, Jesus Christ, until adulthood, I dared ask the Lord to deliver, wash, clean, and lift me.

I desired to be made whole.

Mark 11:24-26 says,

> *"Therefore I say unto you, What things soever ye desire, when ye pray, believe that ye receive them, and ye shall have them. [25] And when ye stand praying, forgive, if ye have ought against any: that your Father also which is in heaven may forgive you your trespasses. [26] But if ye do not forgive, neither will your Father which is in heaven forgive your trespasses."*

Simply put, if we do not forgive others their sins against others, the Father will not forgive our sins. Scripture describes God as infinitely holy – infinitely great, pure, and good. He is completely separated from evil. No one can even come close to His holiness. He is perfectly righteous and just, and sin breaks my line of communication with God. It results in damaging consequences to the soul. It makes me guilty in the Eyes of God. When Jesus speaks to us through His Word and the power He has given us, we have to decide our options. Are You Going to Trust God? Let's look at a miracle through God's Word.

Acts 3:6-7 says,

> *"Then Peter said, Silver and gold have I none; but such as I have give I thee: In the name of Jesus Christ of Nazareth rise up and walk. [7] And he took him by the right hand, and lifted him up: and immediately his feet and ankle bones received strength."*

This is considered a miracle when all the people saw the man leaping and praising God. Everyone marveled at this site because this man was a beggar at the Beautiful Gate of the temple.

Two Questions to ask ourselves:

What do we want from God? Are we willing to make the sacrifices as prescribed to us? Why?

The Season of Reversal' has three things to consider:

1- Return to the Almighty and **repent with Godly Sorrow:**

King David felt the pain of his sin when he slept with another man's wife. It is described as a heavy weight on him. He had a relationship with Bathsheba who was married to Uriah. Then to have her to himself, he murdered Uriah. David was so overwhelmed with the weight of his sin that he cried out to God to have mercy on his soul.

2- Spend time more in **prayer & confession:**

David had experienced godly sorrow with great conviction. He cried out, asking God for forgiveness. He reminded God of His promises. In **Psalm 51**, he wanted to be cleansed, purged, and delivered.

3- Pay your vows:

The Bible teaches us to honor our vows.

Numbers 30:2 says,

"If a man vow a vow unto the Lord, or swear an oath to bind his soul with a bond; he shall not break his word, he shall do accordingly to all that proceedeth out of his mouth."

Keeping your promise to God is paramount. It is better not to make a vow than to go contrary to the will of God. I knew I had to be both 'armed and dangerous.' **I had determined that for God, I live, and for God, I'll die.** Just like I partied and clubbed, I reversed everything. I turned my whole life around. If my heart wasn't right, I had to pray to God. You cannot serve God and His people with an 'unregenerated heart.' I had to rest and allow the Lord to process 'me until I was ready to build and do the work.

If my heart weren't right, I would be bleeding on the people. If the heart is broken and cold, it needs regeneration. **We are double-minded if we have unconfessed bitterness and fake outward show.** Lack of being born again leads to pouring out in the people who look to you. Whatever maladaptive behaviors you have shed onto your Ministry and relationships make it toxic.

When you are tired of walking in sin, cry out to God, *'God, could you make me over.'* Crying out to God is an act of desperation and total concentration. This action is a fervent expression of faith in God and trust in His goodness and power to act on your behalf. Crying out to God expresses the following:

Take the time after you read this page, go to the scriptures, and study them.

GENUINE HUMILITY - Pride makes it difficult to admit that we cannot solve a problem or overcome an obstacle, but it is always true that we need God's help. For, *He forgetteth not the cry of the humble"* **(Psalm 9:12).** (See also **Psalm 10:17.**)

> *"Lord, thou hast the desire: thou wilt prepare their heart, thou wilt cause thine heart, thou wilt cause thine ear to hear."*

UNCONDITIONAL SURRENDER - When a situation becomes so desperate that only God can deliver you, crying out represents total surrender to Him and His ways. Don't try to bargain with Him, He knows you better than you know yourself.

Psalm 66:17–20 says,

"I cried unto him with my mouth, and he was extolled with my tongue. If I regard iniquity in my heart, the Lord will not hear me: But verily God hath heard me; he hath attended to the voice of my prayer. Blessed be God, which hath not turned away my prayer, nor his mercy from me."

A PLEA FOR MERCY - Apart from Jesus Christ, we have no value that merits God's favor. When driven to a point of despair or destruction, your unworthiness before God often becomes more apparent, motivating you to cry out to Him for mercy.

Lamentations 3:22–23 says,

"It is of the LORD's mercies that we are not consumed because his compassions fail not. They are new every morning: great is thy faithfulness."

PERSONAL HELPLESSNESS – Do you understand that you need God's help with only the hard issues and matters of life?

God did not lie when He said in **John 15:5,**

I am the vine, ye are the branches: He that abideth in me, and I in him, the same bringeth forth much fruit: for without me ye can do nothing.

FAITH IN GOD'S POWER AND RESOURCES – It's time to cry out and acknowledge that God is God and that He ability to do what no one else can do.

During the Sea of Galilee storm, the disciples acknowledged Jesus' power to rescue them when they cried out, *"Lord, save us: we perish."* (**Matthew 8:25**).

On January 29, 2021, I accepted a speaking engagement. I was preaching to a room full of radical believers. I had a charge in my heart. After I cried out to the Lord. The Lord showed me that I had a *'murderous spirit'* lingering in me. The behavior, actions, and choices needed to be aligned to position me for God's use, not ours.

I walked around with a nine-millimeter in my purse, house, or anywhere to be ready to fight any time and settle matters. I had to open up to God and put down my weaponry. Also, I shared with the congregation about coming clean with God. Men will see your light. They can even tell where a person's heart is by what they do not say. It's about having conviction. Yes, I wanted to be loved by a man, but I had to find myself first. I can surely do without the violence. My self-esteem was high enough emotionally by this time.

Just like Paul, I have reached the climactic conclusion that anyone who is in union with Christ, by believing His finished work on Calvary paid the price for their sins, has been made a new creation. Trusting that Christ's death, burial, and resurrection are the core of the glorious gospel.

2 Corinthians 5:17 says,

> *"Therefore, if anyone is in Christ, he is a new creature. The old things passed away; behold, things have become new."*

He was preparing me for the newness of life. There wasn't anything troubling about it. If I had an absolute conviction, I would no longer succumb to deceit. The devil will plot and plan against you. Deceit is the ultimate aim. We must be ready to contend with the devil's wiles as believers.

So, all oppression, depression, bitterness, hostility, lying, cheating, anger, and deceitful behaviors get purged out of us. Let God fix it. **Whatever we are exposed to affects us by proxy.** I asked the Lord to remove every fear and calm the storms in my life and others around me.

1 Corinthians 3:12 says,

> *"Every man's work shall be made manifest: for the day shall manifest because it shall be revealed by fire, and the fire shall try every man's work."*

Serving the Lord would require us to eradicate all roots of rebellion from within us. The way to know God is through obedience. Can you find a way to be closer to God? It is through prayer and supplication.

Prayer saved my life because it gave me direct communication with God. Through His Word, I could go from strength to strength and glory to glory. God is my everything. There is no one like Him.

Giving up people, places, and things is okay.

When I was converted, I turned away from everyone who wanted to lead me astray to present myself before God and follow His direction. I mean, it is a daily walk. In the midnight hour, you will find me prostrate before the Lord praying, praising God who gave me another chance. God, you have given me a favor and spared my life.

Colossians 4:5 says,

"Walk in wisdom toward them that are without, redeeming the time."

When we continue in prayer, it is both fervent and effectual. We honor God by speaking from our hearts to Him. The prayer is earnest.

The now-transformed woman spends time with people, ministering to people, doing hygiene runs, blankets give away, food, and clothing. I find a way to speak to the women and children who may have been in similar situations.

I provide biblical counseling as a Violence Interventionist. One of my assignments is working in Compton, California, where I work with a team of people who provide mentoring to decrease gang activity and violence.

I am now assigned as a Mentor working with at-risk students at Compton High School. Sometimes it isn't easy to work in the community if you don't understand the culture. The youth in certain sections have their own code of language and communication. It makes a difference when you are from the area and can speak to different situations and circumstances.

The women are given sessions to talk about womanhood and transformation. We asked questions and talked intimately with each other about our lives. Moving forward they are allowed to heal, gain strength, and rise up as a woman of faith.

Working with women who may have lost everything is an important part of my ministry. **We are all gracefully broken.** God can make us whole again. I am committed to God by serving His people as an ambassador. I am a servant of the Lord.

Isaiah 60:4 says,

"Lift up thine eyes round about, and see: all they gather themselves together, they come to thee: thy sons shall come from far, and thy daughters shall be nursed at thy side."

The Word of the Lord says to seek Him early, and He will convert the sea in your life. Everything in our lives will begin to flow together.

Psalm 63:1-2 says,

O God, thou art my God; early will I seek thee: my soul thirsteth for thee, my flesh longeth for thee in a dry and thirsty land, where no water is; 2 To see thy power and thy glory, so as I have seen thee in the sanctuary.

Please Note: You need to seek God with your whole heart, and then you will understand how worthy of praise and glory God truly is. Because we owe him our very lives? Therefore, it would be a great idea to cut back on the amount of 'worship' we give to the things of this world and give more worship to God.

I became a true servant of the Lord.

There are significant times when we redeem the time by using every opportunity to witness and teach the Gospel of Jesus. I am a living witness of Jesus Christ. I answered the call on my life. I know through everything that happened to me, I would go into the deep to pull people out.

We also begin to fully understand that God has been our rock and hiding place. In times of trouble, God stands with us and shields us from all hurt and harm. I desire to give back to God by honoring him in every way.

We also begin to fully understand that God has been our rock and hiding place. In times of trouble, God stands with us and shields us from all hurt and harm. I desire to give back to God by honoring him in every way.

Psalm 63:1-8 teaches us that our soul should be satisfied in God.

> *"O God, thou art My God; early will I seek thee: My soul thirsteth for thee, my flesh longeth for thee In a dry and thirsty land, where no water is; To see thy power and thy glory, So as I have seen thee in the sanctuary. Because thy lovingkindness Is better than life, My lips shall praise thee. Thus will I bless thee while I live: I will lift up my hands in thy name. My soul shall be satisfied as with marrow and fatness; And my mouth shall praise thee with joyful lips: When I remember thee upon my bed, And meditate on thee in the night watches. Because thou hast been my help, Therefore in the shadow of thy wings will I rejoice. My soul followeth hard after thee: Thy right hand upholdeth me."*

We also begin to fully understand that God has been our rock and hiding place. In times of trouble, God stands with us and shields us from all hurt and harm. I desire to give back to God by honoring him in every way because of all that He has done for me. The most important thing for me is to be strengthened by the power of the Holy Ghost through prayer. Understanding the strength of the Lord might require us to understand God's authority.

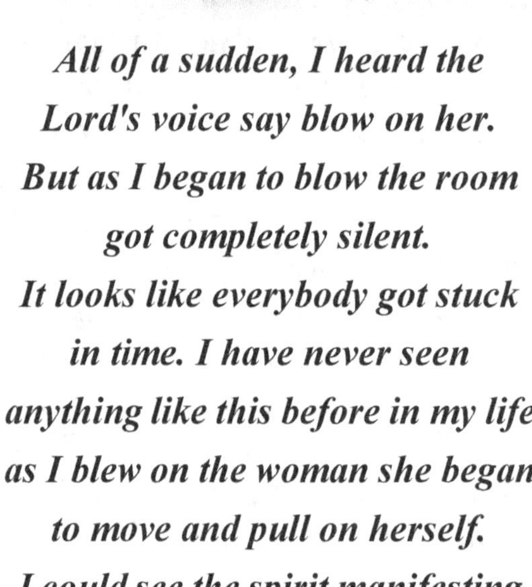

*All of a sudden, I heard the
Lord's voice say blow on her.
But as I began to blow the room
got completely silent.
It looks like everybody got stuck
in time. I have never seen
anything like this before in my life
as I blew on the woman she began
to move and pull on herself.
I could see the spirit manifesting
in her.*

CHAPTER 7

VISITATIONS

I remember my trips to Africa and Jamaica. I was traveling back and forth because I was awed by the signs, healing, and wonders like never before. I saw a man receive healing on his foot. These services were at the school where Pastor Phillips had his ministry. Pastor Phillips asked me to put my hand on his shoulder and pray in my heavenly language.

As I prayed, I saw this boy's foot go in a circle like it had no bone in it. God made it go back to its regular size. It was a true miracle because his foot was the size of a house.

I remember another service at the school when one of the students dropped dead. She was thrown into the building to signify her death. My profession was cardiac technician, so I had an idea of how to proceed in this situation. I looked at the Pastor, signifying that the girl on the floor was dead. Pastor Phillips walked over to her and called her back to life. He asked for her name. She had no pulse.

We began to pray together, and the young girl came back to life. I got down to the floor where she was lying. I could hear her crying. She told me she was sick. I told her the stripes of Jesus healed her. I began to hold her and comfort her. Then her parents came and brought her home.

After this point, I continued to pray and was slain in the spirit. No one had laid hands on me, but someone videotaped it. I was speaking in my heavenly language, and the Lord the people to repent. He said, "Just stop doing what you are doing."

One of the men walked over to me and showed me the video. He said, ***"God is not playing with us. We must repent."***

God was always with me in Africa. There was a time we were at the restaurant where I got burgers. I sat at this table and put my purse under the table. I completely forgot about my purse when the Pastor showed me a bag. We were so immersed in conversation that we left the restaurant.

Pastor Phillips called one of his friends, who was still at the restaurant, to see if he could retrieve my bag. As it turns out, a group of men was sitting at the table, and they declared they had not seen the purse.

I was heartbroken because I had seven thousand in it, plus my passport. I asked God to take care of me. I had a kingdom assignment to fulfill, and nothing was going to interfere with it. God will make a way.

So, we went to an outside prayer service. I began praying for the women. She had my hands and began running backward quickly, and then I spoke firmly, "Let the fire arrest her. The fire of the Holy Ghost had overtaken her, and she dropped to the ground. I have never seen anything like this before. The more I continued the prayer services God gave me spiritual insight.

Soon, I was experiencing visions and dreams in Africa about eagles and angels. The Holy Ghost would lead me to revelations every time I was on the plane. This experience became intrinsic. When I got back to California, I would begin to experience supernatural things at work.

One day, while I was at my work desk in the Emergency room, I had some downtime. I was looking at my bible app on my phone, and the scripture came to me: **Acts 20:24.**

This time, I didn't share the scripture as I read it. Amusingly, I said to myself they better get some Jesus for themselves,

Acts 20:24 tells us,

"But none of these things move me, neither count I my life dear unto myself, so that I might finish my course with joy, and the ministry, which I have received of the Lord Jesus, to testify the gospel of the grace of God."

This scripture set my soul on fire. The Lord revealed to me that my life is worthless, and I must do the work of the Gospel. Paul is saying to us that we must serve the Lord. Our life means nothing to us but to complete our assignment. It confirmed my stand that after all the sum of my experiences, this time now belongs to God. I began praising God quietly. I told everyone to read it for themselves. The Holy Spirit will deal with you as he is dealing with me.

God trained me about scriptures by relaying them to me. This was God's way of purifying me. God tested me to see if I would follow instructions. The man on the gurney was indicating that he recognized what I was doing was coming from the Father.

Anyway, as I sat there, I remember the Paramedics coming in, and it was a homeless person on the gurney, and they sat him by this warmer. The Lord told me to begin to blow, and as I blew, he began pointing his hands up toward heaven, and then he started pointing at me. Then I knew that he knew who I was, and this was a season of signs, wonders, and miracles on supernatural manifestation.

Not long after that, I was working overtime, and I was at the Clark Desk. This was a busy night they were even bringing patients and putting them in the middle of the room to draw blood, and as I stood there at the desk with the clerk, I recognized that Hispanic woman sitting in the middle of the room waiting to get her blood drawn.

Suddenly, I heard the Lord's voice say blow on her. But as I began to blow, the room got completely silent. It looks like everybody got stuck in time. I have never seen anything like this before in my life as I blew on the woman, she began to move and pull on herself. I could see the spirit manifesting in her. The Lord began to show me that she was operating in witchcraft. I blew one more time, and she began moaning and groaning. It was a demonic sound. Then the room light turned back on. Oh, it was so Supernatural.

I remember getting a page to the trauma room one day. It was a 911 to bed one I walked into the trauma room, and I stood there by the door entry waiting for them to call me over to the bedside of the patient because they were trying to revive the patient, and all of a sudden, my hair blew and I heard the Lord so clearly say this will be a sign went to pray for the patient I will blow the wind of God on you one of the nurses who have seen so many things happen to me Nurse Yolanda came over she said, ***I know you're praying. I can look at your face and tell.***

I began to explain to her how the wind blew and how my hair was blowing. She looked at me with a look of wow, and she began to repeat what I said, and suddenly, her hair began to blow. She was so amazed at what had just happened. She said to me, *"Angela, you are Special to God."* Sometimes, it just felt like I lived in a different world. I wasn't normal because God would allow me to see so many different things unexplainably in many ways.

I remember being paged to go to a patient in the hallway, so I walked up to the young man and said, *"I am here to do your EKG."* He looked around me and above my head, saying, *"What is wrong?"* He said, *"What is that big thing behind you?"* I turned around and looked and didn't see anything there. But then I heard a small voice say, *"That's your angel. He is always with you to protect you."* So, I said to the man it's my Angel. He said he sure was big after I was alone doing the EKG. I went back and just cried because I was so grateful to God for what he was doing in my life, work, and overtime.

One night, a nurse who knew me was working back-to-back. She encouraged me to come to the hallway to talk to her first before I did my patient. This lady struggled with adverse behavior. When I entered the room, she put up her fists, and her fists got stuck up in the air, shaking. She said, *"The Lord won't let me hit you."* I said, *"Oh my God."* All of a sudden, she said, *"Can you do the EKG."* I said, *"Yes."*

The lady had an abnormal reading, and I turned it over to the doctor. Nurse Shawn said, *"Something was going on with her heart. That's why she was so adamant about her getting the EKG."* I told the woman it was all God. Everyone at the hospital began to call me a walking Angel in the emergency room.

That day was very tiring, but the Holy Ghost was all over me, and I yielded to it. I received another page to the back room 16-19. When I entered the room, I started setting the patient. There was a man in the hospital bed next to me. He told me my spirit did not agree with my spirit. Suddenly, I started speaking in tongues, and he began projectile vomiting and fell off the bed.

The Nurses came running into the room to see what happened. I exited the room swiftly. The Nurses asked him, ***"What is going on?"*** He responded by shaking his head. He could not speak.

This time, I didn't ask the Lord to reveal the problem. I talked to the Lord about why I was going through so many different things I didn't understand. The Lord told me this was the calling of my life. He revealed to me that I have a deliverance ministry.

I was paged to the psych ward. I went inside the locked door as allowed by the Nurse. Before I set up the procedure process for the EKG, I started talking to the young man. I asked him, ***"How did he end up in this predicament?"*** I went on to ask him, ***"Did he know Jesus?"*** The young man said, ***"I don't believe in Jesus."***

I made a deal with the young man. If he gets a normal EKG, would he then turn his life over to God? He bargained with and agreed to receive salvation. He said, "If have normal, I will serve the Lord." I said, ***"Ok Lord, this one's on you."***

The Lord has never been slack concerning His promises. All God wants is a surrendered life that is committed to serving Him.

We praised and thanked the Lord for His goodness and divine healing. He told me e that he wanted to show me a picture. He went into his room and came back with a drawing pad. He said, *"Let's do it."*

I shared with Him a scripture. The significance is receiving salvation. The first step is accepting the Lord Jesus Christ as your savior. You lay down your life to live for Him. He showed me a picture of an eagle. *"This is spiritual, isn't it?"* Whatever his past experiences were with the church or his belief in Jesus, he never completely gave up hope. When he saw the bountiful greatness of God, it was all he needed to say *"Yes."*

The Lord said to me that sometimes things happen where we once believed God, and after years of going to the altar or being prayed for by the Pastor and nothing changes, we walk away. All satan needs is an open door. In this instance, satan confused his mind.

This young man gave up on life. Everybody in his life had failed him. He was willing to take his life by committing suicide due to major depression.

God proved Himself by letting everyone see the first EKG. Then, the second EKG was normal. This is a miracle of healing for him. God used this miracle as a goal to get him back to God. This was all God.

I realized I was sent to this young man to let Him know God cares about Him. It was not over yet. God needed a willing vessel who wasn't afraid of the young man to minister to him. When he received this miracle from God, he was ready to believe and have faith.

Roman's 10:9 says,

"If thou confess with thy mouth, the Lord Jesus
and shalt believe in thine heart that God raised
Him from the dead, thou shall be saved."

The young man got so excited, saying, *"I believe it. There must be a Jesus somewhere if He did this for me."* Then, he pulled five dollars out of his coat and walked off, saying, *"This must be for you"*. I just stood there smiling, thinking about the gesture. In church, you leave an offering. I turned the money over to the psych nurse upon leaving the ward.

He spoke faith, which brings salvation. He was drawing an eagle, which is symbolic of boldness and spirit, freedom, and self-expression. It was like this young man was searching the darkness for the light. In his mind, he was soaring like an eagle.

Before I left, I told him he needed to read the bible and begin to pray. The Lord will supernaturally change him. The young man said he was going to do it. I told him the angels would be rejoicing that he gave his life to Christ.

I was headed to the cafeteria to get a cheeseburger meal. I reached into my pocket, and I didn't have any money. As I continued walking, a piece of paper was blowing on the floor. I looked at it and a man wearing a white doctor's jacket who said, *"I believe this belongs to you."* When I looked down again, it was five dollars. I looked back up, and the man was gone. Suddenly, I had enough money to get something to eat. God did it for me.

Just to show you, God always supply your needs.

Philippians 4:19 says,

But my God shall supply all your need according to his riches in glory by Christ Jesus.

I began going to church at the Stanfields, with Apostle Donna Spivey. I was so excited about God and what he was doing. I was glad I had Sunday off this week. Church was so fresh and new for me.

Then, that Thursday, I visited Bishop Smith's church for Bible Study. The Bishop was a visitor from New York. When he began preaching, I saw myself going on a journey.

But God was taking me through a Molding and Shaping Process. I was treated as a babe in Christ. I felt it was wrong on every level.

I went through so much. I remember one day, I was speaking in my heavenly language, and I could feel the First Lady of the Church fighting me in the spirit.

The next thing I knew, she died in the service. They were praying for her. Apostle Hawthorne was praying, and nothing was happening. I heard the Lord say go over there and pray. When I laid my hands on her, she jumped up and was crying and looking like she had seen a ghost.

At the time, I didn't realize who I was in God. I just knew I loved God so much I was willing to do whatever God wanted me to do.

It's time for you to take an active step in the battle that God has called and trained you. Stake the borders of your property, community, and government buildings in the community, city, state, and nation. This act faithfully calls out for God to bless the land and rescue His people. It is a declaration that the land was created by Him, of your property, community, city, state, and nation still belongs to Him. It exists for His purposes today. Join our Commander and Chief, our Lord God in this Spiritual Warfare.

CHAPTER 8

SPIRITUAL WARFARE

The most significant part of my learning and development was when I met God, knee bent, and body bowed. I wept all night long and began to speak in my heavenly language.

God asked me, "What are you willing to die for? Was it the men who abused you? I needed that real talk with God about the type of relationships in my life. I needed the Holy Spirit. The abusive men were the strongholds. I never had self-esteem issues, but because I felt good about myself, the men beat me to try to bring me in line. Now my question is not how the Lord sees me, it's Who I am in Him.

To be a disciple of the Lord Jesus the Christ we must be ready and willing to die for Him, that is the cause of the gospel

Ephesians 4:17-19 says,

"This I say, and testify in the Lord, that you should no longer walk as the rest of the Gentiles walk, in the futility of their mind, having their understanding darkened, being alienated from the life of God, because of the blindness of their heart; who, being past feeling, have given themselves over lewdness, to work all uncleanness with greediness."

In **Ephesians 4:17-19**, Paul is instructing the believers of the church in Ephesus on how they are to conduct themselves as believers, who call themselves God's friends.

Some were calling themselves God's friends while acting no different from God's enemies. He admonitions by describing God's enemies' behavior, for them to check their own lives against this and see if they are God's friends.

Spiritual maturity is our goal.

Before we get into *"Spiritual Maturity"*, let's look at how we achieve it. First, we must understand that maturity is where we have grown or developed. The spiritual meaning of maturity means perfected, fully formed, or brought to completion. We don't just arrive at spiritual maturity. It does take time spent in the Word; our devotion becomes a continuous state of development.

Ephesians 4:17 says,

*"The kingdom of God is not meat and drink,
but righteousness, and peace, and joy in the
Holy Ghost."*

We can no longer walk as the rest of the Gentiles, meaning the unsaved and uncommitted hearts to God. Men cannot see the light in us because we blur the lines. Like the Gentiles, we can't say we live a life for God and try to explain to the world how much we are like them. We are to be imitators of Christ.

The Spirit is in direct contact with the Holy Spirit. The Holy Spirit speaks to the Spirit of man. The soul is only supposed to listen to what the Spirit man says.

The Bible says in **James 4:7**,

*'Therefore, submit to God. Resist the devil,
and God will make you free.'*

It is all about choice.

There are three voices in your head. (Holy Spirit, your voice, and the adversary). If you do not have a relationship with God, you will never hear His voice. If the connection is pure flesh, whatever adversity tells you to do, that's what you will do.

When your understanding is darkened, your reality is blurred because you are alienated from God. I couldn't fight the men beating me and the guns. Those men acted in the way they treated me because of their futile thinking and thwarted beliefs.

As believers, we have a higher calling in God. We must spend time getting to know His ways and truth and put off the old man and put on the new man.

To understand the old man and the new man, you need to understand the two following scriptures,

Genesis 1:26 says,

"And God said, let us make man in our image, after our likeness: and let them have dominion over the fish of the sea, and over the fowl of the air, and over the cattle, and over all the earth, and over every creeping thing that creepeth upon the earth."

1 Thessalonians 5:23 says,

"And the very God of peace sanctify you wholly, and I pray God your whole spirit and soul and body be preserved blameless unto the coming of our Lord Jesus Christ."

God said, *"Let us"* (God, Jesus, and the Holy Spirit). The major key to having a productive life in the 'Kingdom of God' is to have a strong spirit like God.

The condition of your spirit will determine the condition of your soul and the quality of your life.

When a person is born-again and makes Jesus the Lord of their life, they must develop and maintain their spirit man in the Word of God; otherwise, they will fall short of everything God has called them to do.

As believers, we must do everything necessary to make sure that our spirit man is strong. As believers who have accepted Christ with their spirit and their mouth (**Romans 10:10**), we should be endeavoring to develop our spirit man to be like the Spirit of Christ.

One who has the Spirit of Christ is one who wins, one who fights, one who has defeated and surpassed all rivals, one who is superior and has all the attributes of a winner.

When we have the Spirit of Christ in us, then and only then can we fight the good fight of faith and experience victory over the adversary. I am running a few minutes late; my previous meeting is running over.

Our spirits should be superior to our minds and bodies rather than being controlled by them. Our spirit man should possess all the attributes of a winner. Our spirits should perfectly embody all that our Lord, our God was when He walked the Earth and all that He still is today.

It is a matter of the heart, soul, and mind. The heart is our spirit man (choice). We want to love God automatically, but our souls are sometimes wounded (hurt).

Our mind needs to assess our behavior, actions, and choice to see if it is aligned with a life committed to God. Men will see your light. They can tell where a person's heart is based on their actions. It is about your conviction to serve God or man.

My main problems started when I looked out the window when I was paralyzed as a young woman, saying I just wanted to go outside and hang out like the other girls. As soon as I was better, I started partying and hanging out. I dressed just like the girls and became them on the party scene.

Do you see the two streams of thought? There is no balance because one hand is holding something (soul), and the other is not of equal yokes. As believers, we do have a new way to walk. It has been stated that Jesus turned us in the right direction, and we have to walk and be processed.

Ephesians 4: 20-24 says,

> *" But ye have not so learned Christ; [21] If so, be that ye have heard him, and have been taught by him, as the truth is in Jesus: [22] That ye put off concerning the former conversation the old man, which is corrupt according to the deceitful lusts; [23] And be renewed in the spirit of your mind; [24] And that ye put on the new man, which after God is created in righteousness and true holiness."*

Strongholds are prevalent in our everyday life mentally, physically, and spiritually. I was spiritually entangled in relationships that were killing me. We struggle to fix what is broken in us.

Domestic Violence seemed to roar through my life. When I heard myself holler out loud, 'I am sick of this and want out.' Then I can move forward with my life. The cycle of violence was destroyed. Let go of the past life. Invite God as your stronghold. Introspectively, I realized the devil was roaring through my life trying to take me out. If any glimmer of your light shines without reinforcements is a target for the enemy to attack you.

2 Corinthians 5:17 says,

> *"Therefore, if anyone is in Christ, he is a new creation; old things have passed away; behold, all things have become new. [18] Now all things are of God, who has reconciled us to Himself through Jesus Christ, and has given us the ministry of reconciliation."*

Ultimately, we have to drop the dead things.

The Word of the Lord says in **2 Corinthians 10:3-6,**

> *For though we walk in the flesh, we do not war after the flesh: [4] (For the weapons of our warfare are not carnal, but mighty through God to the pulling down of strong holds;) [5] Casting down imaginations, and every high thing that exalteth itself against the knowledge of God, and bringing into captivity every thought to the obedience of Christ; [6] And having in a readiness to revenge all disobedience, when your obedience is fulfilled."*

The Lord is truly our strong deliverer.

Psalm 9:9-10 says,

"The LORD also will be a refuge[a] for the oppressed, A refuge in times of trouble. [10] And those who know Your name will put their trust in You; For You, LORD, have not forsaken those who seek You."

I have grown up in grace realizing I wouldn't have survived without God. He is a strong deliverer in a strong city. The enemy seeks to devour us, break down our faith, destroy our minds, and make us weak. God is stronger than anything that comes to us.

2 Samuel 22: 4 says,

"And he said, The Lord is my rock, and my fortress, and my deliverer; [3] The God of my rock; in him will I trust: he is my shield, and the horn of my salvation, my high tower, and my refuge, my saviour; thou savest me from violence. [4] I will call on the Lord, who is worthy to be praised: so, shall I be saved from mine enemies."

Every aspect of your life has to be surrendered.

"He was assured that Jehovah was his God, he expressed that assurance, and he expressed it before Jehovah himself. That had need be a good and full assurance which a man dares to lay before the face of the heart-searching Lord. The Psalmist when hunted by man, addressed himself to God. Often the less we say to our foes, and the more we say to our best Friend the better it will fare with us: if we say anything, let it be said unto the Lord." -Charles Spurgeon (The Treasury of David)

A Prayer of Affirmation

I Am Remarkably Made – **Psalm 139:14 (HCSB)** – *I will praise You because I have been remarkably and wonderfully made. Your works are wonderful, and I know this very well.*

I Will Unashamedly Live For God, Not Man - **Philippians 1:20** – *I eagerly expect and hope that I will have nothing to be ashamed of. I will speak very boldly and honor Christ in my body, now as always, whether I live or die.*

CHAPTER 9

PRAYERS OF AFFIRMATION

Prayers of affirmation are one way of obeying the scriptural command to focus on the things of God.

Philippians 4:8 (Amplified Bible)

> *"Finally, believers, whatever is true, whatever is honorable and worthy of respect, whatever is right and confirmed by God's word, whatever is pure and wholesome, whatever is lovely and brings peace, whatever is admirable and of good repute; if there is any excellence, if there is anything worthy of praise, think continually on these things [center your mind on them, and implant them in your heart].*

Pray on these things.

I humbly thank Prophet Innocent Imogre for praying God's Word over my life. Every day, he sends prayers to my email to help support me on my journey. I would like to share a few of them with you.

I prophesy God's word today; *you'll go out in joy and be led forth in peace; the mountains and hills will burst into song before you, and all the trees of the field will clap their hands; the Lord has blessed you with everlasting blessings, and He will take away from your sickness, poverty, failure, and setback. God will meet you at the point of your need, and all your journey today shall be victorious in Jesus' Mighty Name.*

Psalms 50:10-12 says,

"For every beast of the forest is mine, and the cattle upon a thousand hills. I know all the fowls of the mountains: and the wild beasts of the field are mine. If I were hungry, I would not tell thee: for the world is mine, and the fulness thereof."

I declare the decree: *"all things are working together for"* your good; God will satisfy you with the desires of your heart. He will make you a reference point of success and put a smile on your face. The peak of others shall be your starting point; throughout this day and beyond, God will guide your steps, and His mighty hands will rest on you to single you out for outstanding success and uncommon favor in Jesus' Mighty Name.

Romans 8:28 says,

"And we know that all things work together for good to those who love God and those who are called according to his purpose."

I declare the decree that every evil word spoken against you in the altar of darkness and decision taken against you from the pit of hell shall be scattered by the power of the Holy Ghost. You shall be released as a blessing to your world in Jesus' Mighty Name.

Lamentations 3:36-37 says,

"To subvert a man in his cause, the Lord approveth not. [37] Who is he that saith, and it cometh to pass, when the Lord commandeth it not?"

I pray this morning that as the brightness of a thousand stars cannot stand the glory of a moon, so shall the glory of God in you be celebrated among millions today. The Almighty God will lay His fingers upon everything you touch from today; God will wipe away all tears from your eyes.

It's your day, you will see all spiritual blessings in heavenly places, and you shall experience supernatural abundance from the Lord in Jesus' Mighty Name.

Ephesians 1:3 says,

> *"Blessed be the God and Father of our Lord Jesus Christ, who blessed us with all spiritual blessings in heavenly places in Christ."*

I pray that God will give you a new testimony and promotion this day, week, and month; God begins to magnify you in the sight of all enemies, so they may know that as I was with Moses, I will be with you.

Every malicious intent concerning you shall not prosper again, and you stand upright in this new month. It's well with you in Jesus' Mighty Name.

Joshua 3:7 says,

> *"And the Lord said unto Joshua, This day will I begin to magnify thee in the sight of all Israel, that they may know that, as I was with Moses, so I will be with thee."*

I declare the decree you're fruitful, and you're like a tree planted by the rivers of waters that brings forth its fruit in its season. God will grant unto you whatever your heart desires. I believe doors of opportunity will be re-opened unto you anywhere you knock, and everywhere you go, people will favor you in Jesus' Mighty Name.

Jeremiah 17:7-8 says,

"Blessed is the man that trusteth in the Lord, and whose hope the Lord is.[8] For he shall be as a tree planted by the waters, and that spreadeth out her roots by the river, and shall not see when heat cometh, but her leaf shall be green; and shall not be careful in the year of drought, neither shall cease from yielding fruit."

Revelation 3:8 says,

"I know thy works: behold, I have set before thee an open door, and no man can shut it: for thou hast a little strength, and hast kept my word, and hast not denied my name.".

I declare the decree God blesses you. You're unstoppable in life, for you've received abundant grace and the gift of righteousness. You'll continue to experience unparalleled advantages, unprecedented favor, and prosperity in everything you do today. Rejoice. You're reaping success upon success and reigning in life through Jesus Christ, in Jesus' Mighty Name.

Jeremiah 17:8 (AMP) says,

[Most] *"Blessed is the man who believes in, trusts in, and relies on the Lord, and whose hope and confidence is in the Lord."* (AMP).

As I was commanded, I prophesy that your coast will be enlarged, and grace and favor from God shall encompass and connect you with destiny helpers because your Time of change of level has come today in **Jesus' Mighty Name.**

Ezekiel 37:7, says

"So, I prophesied as I was commanded: and as I prophesied, there was a noise, and behold a shaking, and the bones came together, bone to his bone."

I declare the decree of Isaiah 61:6, you'll eat the riches of the Gentiles, and in their glory shall you boast yourselves, in living God who giveth you richly all things to enjoy in life and good news from a far Country in Jesus mighty Name.

Proverbs 25:24 says,

"As cold water to a thirsty soul, so shall goodness from a far country."

I declare the decree that you have access to untold wealth. Lack and want are not your testimony. You are the seed of Abraham.

Philippians 4:19 says,

"But my God shall supply all your needs according to His riches in Christ Jesus."

I prophesy whatever testimony due for you that the enemy has buried until now, I command it to go back to life; today, the world will hear your testimony in the Name of Jesus Christ.

Revelation19:10 says,

"And I fell at His feet to worship Him. He said unto me, See thou do it not: I am the fellow servant and thy brethren that testimony of Jesus: Worship God: for the testimony of Jesus Christ."

I prophesy by the authority of the Holy Spirit every siege of stagnation, frustration, failure, and dryness expires today. Everything is dead and buried in your life. I caused it to resurrect as you go out today; whatever it will take for you to be successful, Heaven will make it happen in Jesus' Mighty Name.

Ezekiel 37:10 says,

"So, I prophesied as He commanded me, and the breath and spirit came (bones), and they lived and stood up upon their feet, and exceedingly great host." (AMP)

I pray today you shall flourish in your going and coming in because those planted in the house of the Lord shall flourish in the courts of God. You shall still bear fruit in old age as you grow in grace. You shall be fat, advancing in spiritual vitality, and rich in venture(fresh) trust, love, and contentment in Jesus' Mighty Name.

Psalm 92:12 says,

"The uncompromisingly righteous shall flourish like the palm tree be longlived, stately, upright, useful, and fruitful; they shall grow like a cedar in Lebanon majestic, stable, durable, and incorruptible." (AMP)

I declare and decree God will give you a new blessing that will cause everyone to thank God for your life. Something in your life will cause men to gather to celebrate what God has done in you.

Isaiah 43:18 says,

"Behold, I will do a new thing; now it shall spring forth; shall ye not know it? I will even make a way in the wilderness, and rivers in the desert."

I declare the decree that your struggles are over because God has given you everything to enjoy. So that you may know that I am Lord, the God, God has said, I will go before you and level the mountains, to make the crooked places straight; I will break in pieces the door of bronze and cut the bars of iron asunder. I will give you hidden treasures stored in secret places.

Job 22:25-27 says,

" Yea, the Almighty shall be thy defence, and thou shalt have plenty of silver. [26] For then shalt thou have thy delight in the Almighty, and shalt lift up thy face unto God. [27] Thou shalt make thy prayer unto him, and he shall hear thee, and thou shalt pay thy vows."

Triumph In Adversity

" Know ye not that your bodies are the members of Christ? shall I then take the members of Christ, and make them the members of an harlot? God forbid
16 What? know ye not that he which is joined to an harlot is one body? for two, saith he, shall be one flesh.
17 But he that is joined unto the Lord is one spirit.
18 Flee fornication. Every sin that a man doeth is without the body; but he that committeth fornication sinneth against his own body. 19 What? know ye not that your body is the temple of the Holy Ghost which is in you, which ye have of God, and ye are not your own? 20 For ye are bought with a price: therefore glorify God in your body, and in your spirit, which are God's."

1 Corinthians 6:15:15-20

CHAPTER 10

TRIUMPH

The book of Esther is so powerful to me. I've learned to wait on God to do His will in my life. A wise woman sees things from afar and then speaks her case up close. She asked the people to fast and pray as she went before the King. Esther walked in the Authority of God. She believed in the cause to petition the King above all else and not just for herself.

Although Esther had proposed to speak to the king at the first dinner about the assassination, God postponed the meeting and set it further down the road. Esther waited on God's timing. Sometimes, what we desire can be delayed but not denied. God had plans to set a series of circumstances in motion that would bring about justice and glorify Him.

Esther 4: 15-17 says,

"Esther had the people return a message to Mordecai. Then go assemble all the Jews to be found in Shusan and have them fast for me for three days."

When the King asked her what was her request of him? She had determined in her mind that the cost of the people dying and herself was too great a loss. Queen Esther stepped into the King's courtyard; she won his favor. On top of that, King Achashverosh pointed his gold scepter that was in his hand toward Esther. She won his favor. The King granted her request to save Israel and her life.

Hebrews 4:16 says,

"Let us, therefore, come boldly to the throne of grace, that we may obtain mercy and grace to help in the time of need."

We must approach the throne of God's graciousness with confidence and without fear, so we may receive mercy where we missed the mark. God will intercede. He always covers us who follow after His righteousness. At the appointed time of need, an appropriate blessing comes right at the moment. I have seen the miraculous signs and wonders before my very eyes.

Esther was a wise woman. She reminded me of my grandmother in so many ways. Esther believed in prayer and fasting. She kept her heart and goals on the kingdom assignment and did not waiver from it. Esther lived to take care of the needs of the people. My grandmother also established a place for the family. A wise woman sees things from afar and then speaks her cause up close. This is pure boldness on several levels. Esther was willing to lose her life to carry out the assignment.

You have to set a strategy to know the wiles of the enemy. She carefully watched to understand the time and place. She asked God, "How do you want me to carry out this plan?"

Obedience and reverence to God can cause us to be successful in life. Ultimately, we can have the desires of our hearts no matter how great or small. Throughout my book, I saw myself growing in the grace of God.

Imaginably, as I continued day to day, I watched my grandmother make leaps of faith. She bought property to take care of the family. She lived in the front house and lived in the second house.

The property created stability in my family, just like learning and trusting the foundation in Jesus Christ. Our grandmother taught us to take care of our property and build on it. We all learned certain values that were instilled in us. As my life with my son started, I got on my feet and started working to care for my first child. As funny as it may seem, we become who is before us. I am my grandmother and mother who raised me. Also, some of my decisions now are based on how I view life. Satan tried to destroy her stories. But I praise God for forbearance.

1 Corinthians 15:58 says,

> *"Therefore my brethren, Be ye steadfast, unmovable, always abounding in the work of the Lord, forasmuch ye know that your labor is not in vain."*

After going through so many storms, I learned to trust God in such a way that I knew I would become unshakable and unmovable. Then, I came out on the winning side.

A year ago, my life changed when the Lord spoke to me and said, 'This is the year of the armor.' The power of the Holy Spirit is within me in all things, I don't leave home without God. My forefront in life was organizing the work and kingdom assignment that God gave me. I truly thank God for my journey because it taught me how to live again.

I remember when I retired from my job. I had no income whatsoever. I received prophecy after prophecy that I would have my television network year after year after year. We have to understand that God will take you through a process to prepare you to carry the weight of what He's placing in your hands.

He already knows that he's going to give it to you. It's just you know that you're ready to receive the Gift and the way that it carries. A lot of times, you want things that we already know that are coming to happen overnight.

We must understand that the process is to prepare us to understand the vision moving forward. It's important to know all the details, how to run it, and how to keep it going. We also need to see what measures we need to take and what steps to take. The Lord pointed out to me the wisdom of Esther.

Understanding what the project is and how finances play a big part in teamwork and a team that will unite with you. The right people around you, such as intercessors and prayer warriors, are a big part of starting your television network. I'm so excited about this project because I know that it will help people in the kingdom get the Word of God out of the gospel of Jesus Christ

We have to do it in various ways so that we bring in the lost sheep. It hasn't been easy going through this process. Sometimes I felt like giving up, or I wasn't going to be able to do it. Sometimes, I felt like I had the right people to help me. I feel like even with all of the favors that I received, I'll be able to make it. These are all the fears that you have to overcome before you step out. Every step of the way, have faith, believing that you can do all things through Christ Jesus, who strengthens you.

You must pray, fast and don't be weary. Stay in your Word to strengthen you every day, believing God is good.

I want to officially invite you to the daughters of the King Television International Network to become one of my programmers to spread the gospel of Jesus Christ.

Ecclesiastes 12:13-14 says,

"Let us hear the conclusion of the whole matter: Fear God, and keep His commandments: for this is the whole duty of man. [14] For God shall bring every work into judgment, with every secret thing, whether it be good, or whether it be evil."

As believers, it enables us to hold on through trials and tribulations. Essentially, God is telling us to be strong in Him. Strength is required for this purpose. I needed to be empowered by setting boundaries in my life. Power is manifested as you embrace the word, and it will work itself out in your daily life. God provides all we need to be victorious. I needed to understand divine strength to resist the enemy.

Vigilance is the only way we can do it. By being strong in Him, which comes from a covenant relationship. God is the ruler of all. In everything we are facing: the street dealer, gang leaders, pimps, and prostitutes know how to set a strategy for conquering their victims.

Blessed is the man who remains steadfast under trial, for when he has stood the test he will receive the crown of life, which God has promised to those who love him.

Ephesians 6: 18-19 says,

"Praying always with all prayer and supplication in the Spirit and watching thereunto with all perseverance and supplication for all saints;[19] And for me, that utterance may be given unto me, that I may open my mouth boldly, to make known the mystery of the gospel."

We have to seek Him daily and allow God to process our lives. Since my life is predestined, I must walk in complete obedience and work, the work of the one who sent us. I am grateful God chose me.

In **John 9:4** Jesus said,

"I must work the work of Him that sent me, while it is day, while it is day: the night cometh when no man can work."

I gave up everything that would hinder me from being a faithful witness to God. I stopped drinking and smoking cigarettes and other vices. God sent His Son into the world to do work for Him. Jesus had responsibilities. His life was to be the primary example for us.

Simultaneously, I began sobbing and laughing because I understood in 'my knower' it was finally clear to me. I went from prayer in crises to a life of worship, prayer, and praise, becoming an effective witness for the kingdom.

Here I became an Advocate for Jesus Christ, serving the people of God.

Colossians 4:2-4 says,

"Continue in prayer, and watch in the same with thanksgiving; Withal praying for us, that God would open unto us a door of utterance, to speak the mystery of Christ, for which I am also in bonds. That I may make it manifest, as I ought to speak."

I needed to be strengthened and stand in the Authority of God.

Romans 13:1 says,

"Let every soul be subject unto the higher powers. For there is no power but of God: the powers that be are ordained of God."

If we lack a prayer life, we have warfare between the power of the enemy and the power of God in the life of the believers. I believe in the power of prayer through faith. The devil will plot and plan against you.

He does not want to see your life devoted to God. We can break the cycle once we recognize the circumstances and abusive behavior. You will walk away and not turn back. You will learn to make effective choices and place good boundaries.'

We are not called to walk in our strength but in His strength, grace, and mercy. God will put a hedge of protection around you. We seek God's help in prayer to become more than a conqueror.

Deceit was the ultimate aim.

The devil wanted to get you sidetracked and confused in your mindset to ambush you in the Spirit. It is emotional for men and all about the rush and sudden assault.

It's funny that as a little girl, I learned to rejoice with thanksgiving no matter how small or great my success. When I was paralyzed, I talked to God about my healing and believed a miracle would come. When I could move my legs, then stand up on my legs and walk across the room, we all gave God the glory for what He had done. As a teenager, I witnessed the power of full-fledged faith and divine healing. The doctors said, "I might never walk again."

It's not over until God says it's over. `I could hear the Lord saying the words of **Colossians 3:12**,

> *"So, as those who have been chosen of God, holy and beloved, put on a heart of compassion, kindness, humility, gentleness, and patience."*

I learned to fight my battles on my knees and pray the Word. The sum of all of my experiences made me surrender to Jesus Christ. God told me in 2022," This was the year of the Armor, for the enemy comes to hurt your soul.

I wanted to be free. *' Be not deceived, for God is not mocked. "* (Galatians 6:7) God had to deliver me from the mindset: of daring somebody to mess with me so I could kill them. So, I could shoot. I was packing. My gun was in my purse. Never will I be in the old situation of being battered and abused by men with no identity.

God's Word is light. It is the trick of the enemy to destroy your character.

I had to put on my war clothes embodied in the likeness of God: Love, peace, joy, and righteousness required me to live with integrity and be a witness to Him. The way to victory over the flesh is thus, **"living, walking, being led by the Spirit."** Our mission is to grow in grace.

2 Peter 3:18 says,

"But grow in grace and the knowledge of our Lord and Saviour Jesus Christ. To him be glory both now and forever. Amen. "

You Have an Adversary – All, not some things, but! ALL THINGS are possible through Jesus, you do, have an adversary who *"walks around like a roaring lion, seeking whom he may devour"* (1 Peter 5:8). Being more than a conqueror in Christ means that you have the power to resist him and stand firm in the faith. By faith ***"I Am More Than A Conqueror"***

We are to grow in grace and the provision of grace moves on in us.

Our lives imparted by grace must be sustained by grace. This is a part of our freedom from strongholds and workers of iniquity. Grace is a continual thing. We must be sanctified by grace.

1- Look at how we stand in grace:

Romans 5:2 (NLT) says,

"Because of our faith, Christ has brought us into this place of undeserved privilege where we now stand, and we confidently and joyfully look forward to sharing God's glory."

2- In rough times God proves that His Grace is sufficient.

Ephesians 1:7 says,

"By whom also we have access by faith into this grace wherein we stand, and rejoice in hope of the glory of God."

WE MUST BE TAUGHT TO BE STRENGTHENED AND
HAVE HOPE IN JESUS.

**3- In Christ, you are gracefully broken. Here, we
are taught, trained, and disciplined by grace.**

1 Titus 2:11-14 says,

*"For the grace of God that bringeth salvation
hath appeared to all men, [12]Teaching us that,
denying ungodliness and worldly lusts, we
should live soberly, righteously, and godly, in
this present world; [13] Looking for that blessed
hope, and the glorious appearing of the great
God and our Saviour Jesus Christ; [14] Who gave
himself for us, that he might redeem us from all
iniquity, and purify unto himself a peculiar
people, zealous of good works."*

**4- The true question becomes, "*Do I want to be
free?*"**

GOD HAS GIVEN THE WORD OF GOD TO DEVELOP
YOU.

We cannot be deceived at this hour. God's Word is life.
We have to know how the devil is coming to taunt us. The
devil has his tactics and snares.

Think about this: The Prophet Samuel was looking for
David. He was looking for the one. Like the enemy, he
searched for the next King with all his tactics. We must look
for the intent in people.

GOD WILL ALLOW US TO DISCERN THE ENEMY IN THE SPIRIT.

The Prophet did not stop until he finished his assignment. The enemy wants to find his next one. We must remember we are not dealing with natural bets in our lives.

The devil has bullets and a gun too.

To maintain my stance, I had to labor in prayer for victory. Once I put on my Armor, God gave me victory. He prepared the way—the peace that I needed I could not obtain through a man. As we say sometimes, he was a good lover, but what about? My body, mind, or beauty? God regenerates us to experience His love, joy, and peace.

He will lead me correctly if I seek the Lord's guidance and direction.

John 14:27 says,

"Peace I leave with you, my peace I give unto you: not as the world giveth, give I unto you. Let not your heart be troubled, neither let it be afraid."good, or whether it be evil."

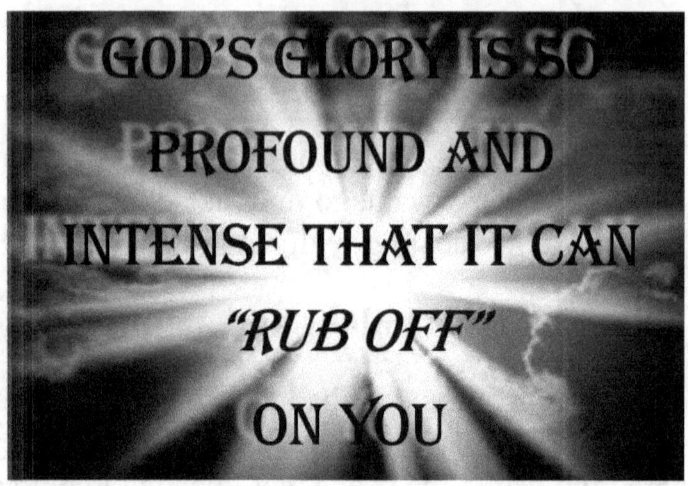

The encounter that **Dr. Angela Roberson** had in this book has given her great joy, hope, and praise for the Lord God. The simple fact that His glory is so profound and intense that it can ***"rub off"*** on the one that's reading this book, you only have to believe. This glory has been a staple of her prayer time for years. That the Lord would allow His light to shine through her to all that she encounters. But many might ask, ***"How do I get this kind of light from God?"*** Well, Moses was of course in direct contact with God Himself in this story so many might say that it's impossible to ***"glow for God"*** today, but I disagree. As Jesus ascended back into Heaven to reign at the right hand of God the Father, He gave the Apostles (us) some great news. Not just great news but world-changing news; for them and every other single person who will ever call upon Jesus as their Lord:

Acts 1:8 says,

"But ye shall receive power, after that the Holy Ghost is come upon you: and ye shall be witnesses unto me both in Jerusalem, and in all Judaea, and Samaria, and unto the uttermost part of the earth."

CLOSING PRAYER

Thank you for the lives that you have prepared beforehand to touch with your word.

Lord, I thank you for the laughter and the wonderful time that we've shared.

.   May all glory and honor come back to you in everything that we do.

God didn't promise a life without pain, struggles, and hardships. He promises to give you the strength to get through them. **Unknown**

James 1:2-4 says,
"My brethren, count it all joy when ye fall into divers temptations; 3 Knowing this, that the trying of your faith worketh patience. 4 But let patience have her perfect work, that ye may be perfect and entire, wanting nothing."

It is in Jesus' name we believe and pray,
Amen.

> ***A praying woman has the credibility and caring spirit to speak of Jesus. People listen to pure love.*** *"The widow who is really in need and left all alone puts her hope in God and continues night and day to pray and to ask God for help"* **(1 Timothy 5:5)**

ABOUT ME

The Prophetess, Dr. Angela Roberson, is known as a Woman of Prayer. She is a California Native and mother of 3 sons: Brian Hilt, Mark Carter, and Angelo Carter. Dr. Angela Roberson is an entrepreneur, a global speaker, the C.E.O, and Founder of Heart 2 Heart Ministries International

Foundation Non-Profit, Heart 2 Heart Food Pantry, and Multi-Purpose Center. Also, the CEO of True Kingdom Records & the television host of

"Prayer Saved My Life."

By the grace of God, she is now the founder of her television network, ***"Daughter of the King TV International Network."*** Angela has her bachelor's degree in biblical studies and counseling. With a push of several great leaders with Godly mentoring and counseling, Dr. Angela Roberson was led to the ministry of prayer and deliverance, where she established her initial center to serve God's people. Heart 2 Heart Ministry International Foundation was birthed in Ghana, Africa, which led her to many other countries: Jamaica, Mexico, and the Bahamas. Dr. Angela Roberson also founded an all-girls school in Pakistan. She has no regrets about answering the call of God; however, by no means has it been easy raising three sons, preaching, teaching, mentoring, and traveling to different states and countries.

Dr. Angela Roberson is a woman of prayer, passion, and integrity who always makes time to pour into others. It is common for her to claim that she would not be able to accomplish her goals without the help of God.

"Trust in the Lord with all your heart and lean not on your own understanding; in all your ways submit to him, and he will make your paths straight" **(Proverbs 3:5-6).**
You only have one life journey; say yes to Jesus. Like Abraham, leave your past with all its entanglements behind. Do not stop halfway

---

MY JOURNEY

Following her sabbatical in Jamaica, she returned home to her church family at the City of Refuge, led by Bishop Noel Jones.

In 1993, she earned her Cardiac Technician License, then worked in the Cardiac registry and worked full time for an L.A. County step-down unit for the mentally ill.

She began working as a Cardiac Technician in the Emergency Room at L.A. County Harbor UCLA Medical Center in 2000.

In 2007, Dr. Angela Roberson received an Administrative Residential Facility (ARF) license for Developmentally Mentally Disabled Adults.

Between 2008 and 2009, she worked for Alondra Homes with level 4(I) clients. Also worked with other sources clients included, but were not limited to, mentally ill, artistic, and disadvantaged children.

Dr. Angela Roberson completed all the requirements for elevation being recognized as a Prophetess to the nation.

In 2016, she received a Humanitarian Award from the Ministerial Alliance Chairman Dr. Mildred Oates at the City of Refuge, under the leadership of Bishop Noel Jones.

In 2016, she was the host of Prayer Saved My Life on the Cross-TV Network to the year of 2021.

Dr. Roberson was a mentor for Sarah's Daughter's young ladies in elementary through high school at the City of Refuge from 2015 to 2017.

From 2017 to 2019, she worked as a public relations representative for Cross T.V. Network.

She earned a bachelor's degree in biblical studies and counseling from Bible Believers College Seminary in 2017 with honors and an award for prayer.

Ministerial Alliance Director Dr. Mildred Oates presented Dr. Roberson with an Award of Appreciation in 2018 at the City of Refuge in Gardena, CA.

In 2021 Dr. Roberson was awarded appreciation for Outstanding Support to Passion to Love and Care Ministries, under the leadership of CEO Founder Prophetess Temika McCanns.

In 2022, the Honorary Doctor of Divinity was awarded to Apostle Roberson.

For the Crossroads organization in 2022, Apostle Roberson was named an ambassador for peace and violence prevention. However, her success does not stop there. Dr. Angela Roberson has been the guest speaker on different local radio and international TV stations such as The Cross-TV Network, OCN Broadcasting, KGLH Radio Station: Motherland Show, and K-Day FM Radio Station. She is also the author of Full Fledge: Understanding the Power of Faith. Dr. Angela Roberson has also been featured in Pastor S.L. Maxwell-Robles Magazine and Level Up Magazine in Paris.

As impressive as Dr. Angela Roberson's accolades sound, her love for God and His people is her drive and the focus of everything that she puts her hands to do. She is a firm believer that promotion ONLY comes from God.

Psalm 75:6-7 God's worshipers of His Kingdom respond with a joyful affirmation of ***His comforting Word*** (v. 6-8). The issue of *promotion* (v. 6), or who is exalted on earth, is determined by God's judgment (v. 7)

> *"⁶ For promotion cometh neither from the east, nor from the west, nor from the south. ⁷ But God is the judge: he putteth down one, and setteth up another. ⁸ For in the hand of the LORD there is a cup, and the wine is red; it is full of mixture; and he poureth out of the same: but the dregs thereof, all the wicked of the earth shall wring them out, and drink them."*